達賴真面目
——玩盡天下女人

True Face of the Dalai Lama
——Playing around with
all women in the world

編著者
白志偉、吳振聲、辛在尊、葉音讚
成種慧、董建昌、吳錫焜

Editors / Authors

Pai, Chih-Wei; Wu, Chen-Sheng; Hsin, Tsai-Tsun; Yeh, Yin-Tsan

Cheng, Chung-Hui; Tung, Chien-Chang; Wu, Hsi-Kun

ISBN 978-986-6431-14-2

屬於政治的還給政治，

屬於宗教的還給宗教。

別把政治扯進佛教內部事務中，

也別以佛教名義參與政治事務。

What belongs to politics should return to politics, and what belongs to religions should return to religions.

Do not bring politics into the internal affairs of Buddhism, and do not participate in the political affairs under the name of Buddhism either.

本書為您揭開

達賴喇嘛的真面目

內容精彩，不容錯過

In this wonderful book,

you will find the true face of the Dalai Lama.

Do not miss it!

綠帽疑雲？

假使您不想戴綠帽子，請記得詳細閱讀此書；假使您不想讓好朋友戴綠帽子，請您將此書介紹給您的好朋友。

假使您想保護家中的女性，也想要保護好朋友的女眷，請記得將此書送給家中的女性和好友的女眷都來閱讀。

財團法人 正覺教育基金會

Are you a cuckold?

If you do not want to be cuckolded (to wear a green hat in Chinese slang), do remember to read through this book; if you do not want your good friends to be cuckolded, please introduce this book to them.

If you want to protect the females of both your family and your good friends, please do remember to give them this book for reading.

True Enlightenment Education Foundation

香格里拉的真相

爲什麼千年大騙局還能繼續存在這個世間？爲什麼穿紅衣的喇嘛們最後會使學密女人的丈夫戴上綠帽子？密宗的修行爲什麼自始至終以男女交合作爲修行的法門？爲什麼男人與妻子共同學密以後會失去妻子？爲什麼女人不阻止丈夫學密就會失去丈夫？爲什麼達賴喇嘛的祈福是無效的？在這本書中都將爲您詳細說明。讀了此書可以瞭解密宗雙身法的本質，幫助家中的女眷遠離喇嘛的性侵害。

財團法人 **正覺教育基金會**

The Truth about Shangri-La

How can the big millennial fraud still exist in this world? How can the lamas, who wear red robes, cuckold those men whose wives are learning the Tantric practice? Why does the Tantric practice use copulation as its practice method all the time? Why will a man lose his wife if both of them are the Tantric learners? Why will a woman lose her husband if she does not prevent her husband from learning the Tantric practice? Why is the Dalai Lama's prayer useless? You will find all the detailed answers in this book. Through this book, you can fully understand the essence of the Couple-Practice Tantra in Tibetan Buddhism, and thus help your female family members be away from the sexual assaults by the lamas.

True Enlightenment Education Foundation

編　者　序

　　密宗這十年來不斷地強調**博愛**，這是人間至善的名詞。但密宗所說的博愛，卻另有意涵，並非社會人士所知。由於不知密宗倡言博愛的真正用意，社會大眾與新聞媒體只在所見的表相下，以為密宗高唱博愛是善心的宗教行為，於是共同讚揚支持之。

　　但密宗所謂的博愛，其實只是假**博愛**之名，行其淫人妻女之實的惡行。密宗高唱博愛的背後真相，是男女交合追求從男根遍及全身的樂受，是奉行宗喀巴《菩提道次第廣論》中的「止觀」雙身法內容。這些「止觀」的內容全是男女合修的雙身法，但是用詞極隱晦，只有喇嘛們知道，不對一般信徒說明。喇嘛們只對被他們看上的女性，私底下教導這些「止觀」，目的是要誘惑她們上床合修雙身法。宗喀巴要求喇嘛應該每天都與女人合修雙身法，每天追求的是：要將從男根生起的樂受擴大到全身，而且時間必須持久。宗喀巴要求喇嘛們必須每一世的每一天都與女人交合，而且要每天十六小時都抱著女人保持全身遍樂。

　　由這個事實便知道密宗大力倡導博愛的原因，是要**愛盡天下女人**；只要是他們看上的具有姿色的女人，就要設法一一與之交合，使自己每天可以遍身大樂，也要使與他們交合的所有女人都獲得遍身大樂，這就是密宗高唱**博愛**的真正意涵。然而密宗對這種意涵從來都不明講，只是含糊其詞而高

Editorial Note

Over the recent decade, Tibetan Buddhism has continuously emphasized the concept of **"love for all"**, which is a well-known virtue. However, the "love for all" referred to by Tibetan Buddhism has a different meaning than the one known by the public. Unaware of its actual meaning, the public and news media can only deduce from the outer appearance that the promotion of "love for all" by Tibetan Buddhism is a virtuous religious behavior and thus generally admire and support their religious movement.

However, the so-called **"love for all"** by Tibetan Buddhism is in fact the evil behavior of having sex with others' wives or daughters, in the guise of "love for all". The truth about this "love for all" promoted by Tibetan Buddhism is the pursuit of tactile happiness extending from the male sexual organ to the whole body during copulation; this practice follows the teaching of the Couple-Practice Tantra, which is the contents of Tranquility and Insight in Tsongkhapa's book *The Great Treatise on the Stages of the Path to Enlightenment*. All contents of Tranquility and Insight are about the co-practice of copulation by a male and female couple. Due to the book's obscure wording, only the lamas can grasp its real meaning, which they do not explain to general believers. They only teach these "Tranquility and Insight" tricks in private to the females they are interested in, with the purpose of seducing them into cultivating the couple-practice of copulation. Tsongkhapa requested the lamas to cultivate the Couple-Practice Tantra every day and, during practice, to extend the tactile bliss from the sexual organ to the whole body for a long time. He requested that they should copulate with women every day in each lifetime and should maintain the whole-body tactile bliss by embracing women for at least sixteen hours a day.

From the above facts, we can conclude that the purpose for Tibetan Buddhism to extensively promote "love for all" is in fact to **love all women in the world**. Whenever they find a qualified beautiful woman, they will make every effort to copulate with her so that both

唱**博愛**，讓社會人士與新聞媒體不知究裡，只能從表面上誤認他們是很有愛心的宗教，於是大力加以支持，認為是共同引導社會走向良善與光明，事實上卻造成更多學密家庭支離破碎。

　　由於這是事實而社會人士及新聞媒體普皆不知，凡是知其真相者都應對社會人士加以說明，使密宗倡導**博愛**的真相普令社會大眾週知，以免更多女性繼續受害（與喇嘛發生性關係而喪失了貞節），防止學密家庭支離破碎的慘事繼續發生。由此緣故，發行本書，期望社會大眾了知密宗倡言**博愛**的真相，是為序。

2010 年 1 月 5 日

parties can obtain the whole-body bliss. This is the truth about **"love for all"** promoted by Tibetan Buddhism. However, Tibetan Buddhism has never disclosed it, but instead, has just been hawking the expression **"love for all,"** a concept that they fail to explain clearly, so that the public and news media, due to misconception, would wrongly think that it is a religion with love and would thus zealously support it. The public and news media think their behavior is to generally guide the society toward virtuousness and brightness, but in fact they destroy more families of Tantric learners.

Because these are the facts that the public and news media are unaware of, all those who know the truth should speak up and unveil the truth about the **"love for all"** promoted by Tibetan Buddhism to the public. Therefore, we can prevent more females from being hurt continuously (losing their chastity due to having sex with the lamas) as well as the occurrence of family disruptions. For these reasons, we publish this book with the hope that the public can learn the truth about the **"love for all"** promoted by Tibetan Buddhism, and thus make this note.

January 5, 2010

目　　錄

Contents

前　言

　　「博愛」一詞乃是常常聽到的說法，甚至許多宗教人士都以博愛爲口號，但是這些「博愛」講法的背後，其目的到底是什麼？這個問題乃是大家必須特別注意的，因爲從古時到現代社會進行詐騙的集團很多，宗教界也不例外；我們瞭解到，每年都有宗教性侵的事件爆發，背後還沒有被揭露的更不計其數；這些口口聲聲喊著「博愛」的人，有很多乃是包裝成各種的方式而展現在世人的面前，其中以達賴喇嘛爲首的藏傳「佛教」─密宗喇嘛教─就是一個很好的例子。達賴喇嘛在〈二○○六年達賴喇嘛的祝福──生活方針〉中說得很好聽：「**愛和烹飪之道即在恣情任性而爲。**」[1] 他這句話背後隱藏著什麼內涵呢？我們將會慢慢的解析這位藏傳「佛教」─喇嘛教─最高法王所弘揚「無上瑜伽」背後的核心思想。

　　我們看到近二、三十年來，密宗喇嘛教漸漸入侵寶島台灣，各地藏密共修中心如雨後春筍般地紛紛設立，他們都號稱是「藏傳佛教」，用「佛教」之名義，實際上所弘揚的內涵卻是古印度性力派雙身修法生殖崇拜的喇嘛教。因爲台灣人民普遍善良，而且台灣佛教界人士普遍對於達賴喇嘛爲首的藏傳「佛教」─喇嘛教─弘法的實質內涵不清楚，因此沒有能力分辨喇嘛教在教理上、法義上、修行上的本質，其實是與佛法無關；並且這些藏傳「佛教」的宗旨內涵，都與眞正的佛教相牴觸。但是台灣民眾因爲不知道他們的底細，所以接受了「西藏密宗就是佛教」的錯誤認知，以

---

[1] 英文原文爲：Approach love and cooking with reckless abandon.
　資料來源：http://eternity.why3s.net/redirect.php?goto=newpost&tid=589
　下載時間：2009/10/23

Preface

The term "love for all" has been heard frequently, and many religious people use it as a slogan. However, what are their real purposes behind the term for "love for all?" We must pay special attention to this question because there have been many defrauding groups from the ancient time till nowadays, without exception in the religious society. We realize that there are many religious sexual assaults disclosed every year, with other countless cases undisclosed yet. Many of those people who frequently say "love for all" disguise themselves in different ways with different outer appearances in front of the public. Among them, the most real case is Tibetan "Buddhism," or called the Tantric Lamaism, led by the Dalai Lama. He says gracefully in *The Blessing of the Dalai Lama on 2006—Instructions for Life:* "Approach love and cooking with reckless abandon."[1] What is the real meaning behind this statement? We will gradually expound the kernel thought behind "the Highest Yoga Tantra," which is propagated by this highest dharma-king of Tibetan "Buddhism"—Lamaism.

In recent twenty to thirty years, we can see that the Tantric Lamaism penetrates Taiwan gradually; the cultivation centers of the Tantric practice have been set up very quickly in Taiwan, in the name of "Tibetan Buddhism." Under the guise of "Buddhism," they are in fact spreading the doctrine of Lamaism, which originates from the ancient Hindu Tantrism with reproduction worship and cultivates the Couple-Practice Tantra of copulation. Because of Taiwan people's virtue and the Taiwan Buddhist society's ignorance of the Tibetan Buddhism's real contents, the public do not have the capability to identify that the essence of the Lamaistic teachings, doctrines, and practices in fact have nothing to do with the Buddha dharma; the gist of Tibetan "Buddhism" even conflicts with the teachings of the real Buddhism. Due to the ignorance of their real details, Taiwanese people accept the misconception that "Tibetan Buddhism is Buddhism," wrongly think they are the venerable monks with pure practice, and thus donate huge money to offer these lamas, who diligently cultivate the Couple-Practice Tantra of copulation. Therefore, these lamas and *rinpoches,* who were exiled to many countries, all choose Taiwan as the best place where they want to come for dharma transmission and empowerment. They all think that Taiwanese people are very rich. Taiwan

---

[1] Citation resource: http://eternity.why3s.net/redirect.php?goto=newpost&tid=589
Download time: 2009/10/23

爲喇嘛們都是修行清淨的高僧，因此每年都願意捐輸大筆金錢來供養這些勤修雙身法的喇嘛；所以這些流亡各國的喇嘛、仁波切們，都以到台灣弘法灌頂爲第一志向，都認爲「台灣錢淹腳踝」，所以台灣小島儼然成爲支助達賴爲首的藏密流亡政府之最大財源。這些以修雙身法爲宗旨的喇嘛們不僅帶走台灣人的血汗錢，更染指許多台灣女性，展現他們認爲的「博愛」—— 要與所有女性都合修無上瑜伽雙身法。我們可以看到在台灣各地的藏密共修中心，常常有婦女遭受喇嘛性侵的事件發生；而且還是層出不窮，能夠在媒體上面報導的其實很有限；大多數的性侵事件都爲了名節的考慮而被隱藏起來了，而被媒體報導出來的永遠都只是無數案例中的極少數。

密宗喇嘛們不僅假冒佛教名義，甚至已經造成社會上的亂象；這些亂象的主要根源，在於喇嘛教的核心教義—無上瑜伽樂空雙運—就是以能長時間專注於男女性高潮中一念不生，說這就是最高層次無上瑜伽的樂空不二、樂空雙運的證量，欺騙佛教徒說這樣就是證得佛果而成佛了；妄說透過男女性交（美其名爲無上瑜伽灌頂）可以提升心靈的純淨，因此吸引許多不知密宗喇嘛教底細的無知者及無辜者。所以這些打著藏傳「佛教」名號的喇嘛們每年都有許多活佛、仁波切來到台灣進行所謂的灌頂、祈福、弘法之活動，透過各種政治、新聞、商業媒體等宣傳手段，用高明的騙術來騙取台灣女子與其合修雙身法；美其名說這些女性是佛母，使她們認爲與活佛上師合修雙身法即能快速成就佛法。由於喇嘛們這樣的說法，已經使部分台灣女性迷惑於佛母這個虛有的名號，甘願與這些號稱「活佛」的喇嘛們，共同邪淫與斂財，並且串通來共同欺騙不知情的更多台灣女性；等而下之者，就以加持修行爲藉口，直接性侵具

becomes the biggest financial supporter to help the exiled government of Tibetan Buddhism, which is led by the Dalai Lama. These lamas, who practice the Couple-Practice Tantra, not only take Taiwanese people's hard earned money away but also have sex with many Taiwanese females, presenting their "love for all"—to cultivate the Couple-Practice Tantra of the Highest Yoga Tantra with all females. We can see many sexual assaults happen over and over again at many Tantric cultivation centers in Taiwan. The cases that were reported by the media are in fact very few; most of the sexual assaults were covered up out of consideration for the victims' reputation.

The Tantric lamas not only steal the name of Buddhism but also have created social chaos. The major cause of social chaos results from the kernel doctrine of Lamaism—the Dual Operations of Bliss and Emptiness through the Highest Yoga Tantra—which concentrates on the orgasm and keeps a state where no thought arises for a long time. They claim that this is the realization level of the Union of Bliss and Emptiness as well as the Dual Operations of Bliss and Emptiness, which is the highest achievement in the Highest Yoga Tantra. They cheat the Buddhists by saying that this level is the realization of the ultimate Buddhahood, and one is able to further purify the spirit through sexual intercourse (dignifying it with the name of empowerment of the Highest Yoga Tantra). By this way, they attract many of those who are innocent and ignorant of the real contents of the Tantric Lamaism. Consequently, many lamas, living-buddhas and *rinpoches,* in the name of Tibetan "Buddhism," come to Taiwan to hold the activities like empowerment, prayer or dharma-spreading through the advertising methods of politics, news and media business to cheat Taiwanese females for couple-practice of copulation. Lamaism names these females buddha-mothers and makes them wrongly think they will become a Buddha quickly if they can have the couple-practice of copulation with their living-buddha teachers (gurus). With that kind of claims, some Taiwanese females who have been confused with the illusory title of buddha-mother are willing to cooperate with the lamas on sexual misconduct as well as cheating, and collude with them to cheat more innocent females. The worse case of the lamas' behavior is using the excuse of enhancing the practice to directly rape the beautiful female followers to satisfy their sexual desires through the Couple-Practice Tantra; they make these females, who want to learn the pure Buddha dharma originally, fall into the endless sufferings but dare not to disclose it at all. The Tantric lamas who worship this kind of "love for all" advocated by the Dalai Lama and want to love all women in the whole world are in fact hoping to cultivate the Couple-Practice Tantra

有姿色的女信徒，將台灣的女性做爲其修雙身法洩慾的工具；致令許多本來想要修學清淨佛法的婦女，從此陷入無盡的苦難中，卻又不敢聲張。密宗喇嘛們崇奉達賴喇嘛倡導的這種「博愛」，想要愛盡一切的女人，其實是希望與天下所有女性都合修雙身法，這才是達賴提倡「博愛」的眞正意思，但社會大眾都被他所騙，不知道應該提防家中的女性受害。除了這些女性同胞被性侵之外，更可憐的是這些女性的丈夫們，已經被暗地裡戴上綠帽子了，還要奉上大把大把的鈔票供養喇嘛，這是多麼可憐悲哀的事情。更有許多人是賠了夫人又折兵，暗地裡流下男人的眼淚，卻無處控訴。而且這些事情依舊在台灣各地陸續發生。台灣如是，大陸乃至全球莫不如是；所以藏傳「佛教」—喇嘛教—用佛教的外表、媒體的宣傳、政治的手段、人權的口號來包裝，藉以達到他們「博愛——愛盡天下的女人」的目的。

　　台灣是自由民主且理智的社會，言論自由而不受限制，所以密宗可以大聲發言蠱惑台灣民眾；但許多人不知道這些號稱藏傳「佛教」的喇嘛教根本不是佛教，因此讓這些假冒佛教名義的雙身修法者，繼續性侵我們善良無知的女性。正覺教育基金會以教化民心、維護善良風俗爲職志，致力於弘揚 釋迦牟尼佛的如來藏法，以清淨修行邁向成佛之道爲目標。不忍見到這些假冒佛教名義的喇嘛們戕害百姓，因此提出呼籲，希望大眾能夠認清藏傳「佛教」—喇嘛教—的底細。本來藏傳「佛教」—喇嘛教—在古時候資訊不發達，因此都是秘密修雙身法，而男女性交雙修乃是喇嘛教的本質，也是根本而且始終一貫的教義，然而大部分人都不知道這個事實，初學密宗的人也不知道這個眞相。但是現代社會資訊發達，喇嘛們又大批來台淘金開示，慢慢洩漏底細；而且這些

with worldwide females. This is the true meaning of the Dalai Lama's "love for all." However, the public are defrauded by him and do not know that they should prevent their female family members from harm. In addition to those females who are sexually assaulted, their husbands are even more pitiful; they have been cuckolded secretly, but they still offer lots of money to the lamas. What a pity! Many of them even lose their wives and money at the same time, and can only weep in private, nowhere to accuse the lamas. These events continue to happen everywhere in Taiwan, China, and even the whole world. By this way, Tibetan "Buddhism"—Lamaism—uses the Buddhist appearance, media advertisement, political manipulation, and the slogans of human right to dignify themselves so that they can "have love for all women in the whole world."

Taiwan is a free, democratic, and rational society that allows the freedom of speech. Therefore, Lamaism can speak loudly in public to cheat Taiwanese people. Many people do not know that Lamaism, or so-called Tibetan "Buddhism," is not Buddhism at all and let the lamas, who disguise themselves as the Buddhists and practice the Couple-Practice Tantra, continue to sexually assault our virtuous, ignorant females. The True Enlightenment Education Foundation commits itself to the social education and the guarding of virtuous custom, and aims to spread Buddha Sakyamuni's Tathagatagarbha dharma as well as to purify the practice for the way to Buddhahood. The Foundation cannot bear to see the lamas, who disguise themselves as the Buddhists, harm people; therefore it appeals to the public with the hope that they can recognize the details of Tibetan "Buddhism"—Lamaism. Due to poor information availability in ancient time, originally Tibetan "Buddhism" practitioners cultivated the Couple-Practice Tantra in secret, and so most of people did not know that the couple-practice of copulation is the essence of Lamaism and the root, consistent doctrine; even the novice Tantric practitioners did not know this truth either. However nowadays, with the well-developed information and the teachings of the lamas who visit Taiwan, the real details of the Tantric practice are disclosed gradually. In addition, since more and more sex scandals about the lamas are uncovered, many wise people can gather the real evidence and announce it to the public. But until now, lots of people still do not know the truth. As for the Dalai Lama, who is the leader of Tibetan "Buddhism," he does not blame the lamas for the more and more sexual assaults but rather quietly support them. In fact, it is impossible for him to disagree with them because the Couple-Practice Tantra is the root doctrine of the Tantric practice. In the Dalai Lama's writings, we also find many statements that promote the Couple-Practice Tantra. The kernel doctrine of

喇嘛們性醜聞的事蹟又愈來愈多被揭發，因此讓許多有智者能夠舉出現實證據，公諸於世。但是社會大眾還是有很多人不知道，而我們看藏傳「佛教」的首領—達賴—對於層出不窮的雙身法性侵事件，不但不加譴責，反而默默支持；因爲密宗實際上就是以雙身法作爲根本教義，達賴當然不可能反對。我們也於達賴的許多著作中找出很多鼓吹雙身法的說法，因爲藏傳「佛教」教義的核心本質，就是講求雙身法的淫樂技術——永不洩精而能保持長時間的堅挺，所以美其名爲金剛；長時間享受性愛的快樂，美其名爲證得**報身佛**，其實只是「**抱身**」佛，與佛法中的**報身佛**境界完全無關。因此於達賴喇嘛中文或英文的書中多次談到性交行爲可以得證瑜伽，主張佛法的實證要透過性交來修行；達賴這樣公開教導鼓勵修雙身法，把欲界最低層次的師徒男女輪座雜交的邪淫亂倫法，謊說爲佛法的最高修證，當然不會制止喇嘛們對女信徒誘姦或性侵害。達賴喇嘛又透過政治的手段來宣傳作秀，美其名爲祈福、灌頂、自由和平……等。他這樣的作法包裝，就是想要爲藏傳「佛教」—喇嘛教—進行雙身法的合理化而已，實質上他們的作法還是喇嘛與女信徒——苟合邪淫的行爲。達賴喇嘛巧妙的運用很多花招來矇騙世人，他的說法不可能欺矇有智慧與理智的人；但是仍有許多迷信表相的人會被「轉世活佛」的說謊行爲所矇騙，致使部分誤信奉達賴喇嘛爲大修行者的台灣佛教出家人，亦違犯 釋迦牟尼佛的清淨教導—出家人應終身不淫—的清淨無欲戒律，誤以爲密宗的雙身法也是佛法，因此有些出家人早已暗中廣修雙身法，嚴重違犯戒律，成就地獄業種，這都是被達賴喇嘛集團所害的可憐人。想想這影響將何其深遠：連在家居士都不會違犯不邪淫的戒條，但出家人竟然都被達賴誘惑而無法遵守清淨戒律，這些信受藏傳「佛教」—喇嘛教—的出家人，如今都

Tibetan "Buddhism" is the obscene skill of the Couple-Practice Tantra—having a stiff erection without ejaculation for a long time, thus *vajra* being called, and enjoying sexual happiness for a long time, thus the reward-body buddha being realized. Actually this kind of **reward-body** buddha is the "**embracing-body**" buddha and has completely nothing to do with the state of the real **reward-body** Buddha in Buddhism. Therefore, the Dalai Lama, in his many writings of both English and Chinese, talks about the realization of yoga through copulation and proclaims that the actual realization of Buddhism should be practiced via sex. He teaches and encourages people to practice the Couple-Practice Tantra in public, and lies that the obscene sexual behavior among the teacher and students in turn, which is the lowest level in the desire-realm, is the highest Buddhist practice and realization. With this kind of teachings, of course he does not forbid the lamas to either seduce or rape their female followers. Through the political advertising means, the Dalai Lama dignifies his thoughts with the name of prayer, empowerment, freedom, peace, etc. in order to rationalize the Couple-Practice Tantra of Tibetan "Buddhism." Essentially their actual behavior is still the obscene sexual intercourse between the lamas and the female followers. Although the Dalai Lama skillfully uses many tricks to cheat the public, the wise and rational people will not be tricked by his lies. Nevertheless, many other people who blindly believe in the outer appearance of the "reincarnated living-buddha" are deceived by his lies. Some Taiwanese Buddhist monastic practitioners who wrongly believe that the Dalai Lama is a great practitioner, with a misconception that the Couple-Practice Tantra is the Buddha dharma too, violate Buddha Sakyamuni's pure, clean precept of celibacy for monastic persons and have cultivated the Couple-Practice Tantra in secret already. They seriously violate the precept and have committed the sin of hell karma. Such poor people are the victims of the Dalai Lama's group. Just think about how influential it is: Even the lay Buddhists will not violate the precept of no sexual misconduct, now the monastic practitioners, with the Dalai Lama's enticement, cannot keep their precept of celibacy and continue to extensively cultivate the Couple-Practice Tantra in secret; with this situation, the moral virtues will completely disappear, and the traditional ethics will no longer exist in Taiwan; inevitably, the same thing will also happen in China. Therefore, every man should prevent his wife from learning the Tantric practice lest he will be cuckolded unwittingly, and every self-respecting female should keep far away from the Tantric practice so that she can be free from the doubts of her friends and husband for having sex with the lama.

還在暗中繼續廣修雙身法，那台灣未來的道德將淪喪殆盡，傳統倫理亦將蕩然無存。台灣如此，大陸當然也無法避免；所以一切男人都應該阻止妻子修學密宗，免得被喇嘛們暗中戴了綠帽子而仍然不知；潔身自愛的女性也應該遠離密宗，以免被親友及丈夫懷疑是否曾經與喇嘛上過床了。

其實從佛法實證的角度來看，達賴喇嘛只是一介凡夫，根本未斷我見（沒有證得初果），更未開悟明心（不是證悟的菩薩），只因為在西藏地區透過政治運作的愚民政策而穿鑿附會，標榜是觀世音菩薩的轉世；現在又透過西方媒體的大肆渲染，才被大家所尊崇恭敬。但理性的人試想一個問題：**如果達賴喇嘛真的是觀世音菩薩的轉世，觀世音菩薩會教導徒眾要修學男女性交的雙身法，而每天保持長久的淫樂嗎？甚至師徒、母子、父女互相亂倫的輪座雜交嗎？難道觀世音菩薩會這麼不清淨嗎？**有些喇嘛連母性畜生都不放過，要與這些動物修雙身法。宣稱是觀世音菩薩轉世或化身的達賴喇嘛，竟然認同喇嘛們如此胡來，而自己也這樣教導密宗的喇嘛們，他有可能是清淨而超越欲界、色界、無色界的觀世音菩薩的轉世或化身嗎？

再試想下面的問題：**大慈大悲的觀世音菩薩會率眾吃肉、飲酒嗎？會教導徒眾要以五甘露**（大香〈大便〉、小香〈小便〉、腦髓、經血、精液）、**五肉**（象肉、馬肉、人肉、豬肉和狗肉等五種帶血的生肉）**來祭祀清淨無染的佛菩薩嗎？**

因此，稍有理智與佛法知見的人都知道：這根本不是觀世音菩薩的清淨境界，觀世音菩薩根本不可能這樣做，因為那已經違背佛法的基本戒律，也是下墮於欲界法中。再從另外一個角度來

From the aspect of Buddhist actual realization, in fact, the Dalai Lama is just an ordinary person who neither eliminates the self-view (not realizing the First Fruit yet) nor gets enlightened (not an enlightened bodhisattva). He deceitfully claimed to be the reincarnation of Bodhisattva Avalokitesvara through the deliberate political manipulation in Tibet and is highly praised and respected by the public now through the gross exaggeration of the western media. But a rational person can think over the following questions: If the Dalai Lama were the real reincarnation of Bodhisattva Avalokitesvara, would Bodhisattva Avalokitesvara teach the disciples to cultivate the Couple-Practice Tantra of copulation so that they can keep the obscene happiness longer every day? Does the practice allow the copulation of incest between teacher and student, mother and son, or father and daughter? Is that possible that Bodhisattva Avalokitesvara is so unclean like this? Some lamas even have sex with female animals to cultivate the Couple-Practice Tantra. Surprisingly, the Dalai Lama, who claims himself to be the reincarnation or embodiment of Bodhisattva Avalokitesvara, agrees with the lamas' infamous behavior, and he himself teaches them to do so as well. Is it possible that he is the reincarnation or embodiment of Bodhisattva Avalokitesvara, who is clean, pure, and beyond the desire-realm, form-realm and formless-realm?

Some more questions are: Is it possible that Bodhisattva Avalokitesvara, who has great compassion, eats meat and drinks alcohol with his followers in public? Would he teach his followers to offer the five kinds of nectar (feces, urine, brain marrow, menses and semen) and the five kinds of flesh (elephant flesh, horse flesh, human flesh, pork and dog flesh with blood) to the pure, clean, undefiled Buddhas and bodhisattvas?

Those who have sense of reason and the Buddhist knowledge all know: This is by no means the clean, pure state of Bodhisattva Avalokitesvara; Bodhisattva Avalokitesvara never does that kind of thing since it has violated the basic precept of the Buddha dharma and fallen down into the dharma of desire-realm. One can think about it from another aspect: If the Dalai Lama is the true reincarnation of Bodhisattva Avalokitesvara, why is he unable to realize the basic First Fruit of the Liberation-Way? Why is he unable to get enlightened and attain the merits and virtues of seeing the way of the Buddhahood-Way? He does not even have the merits and virtues of seeing the way, not to mention the wisdom of practicing the way, which the bodhisattvas of the various grounds have.

思考：如果達賴喇嘛真的是觀世音菩薩的轉世，爲何連解脫道最基本的初果都無法證得？爲何還不能開悟明心而無法證得佛菩提道的見道功德？連見道的功德都沒有，就更別說是諸地的修道智慧了。

　　然而這樣的事實擺在眼前，全然是凡夫的達賴竟然還厚顏無恥地縱令徒眾，向不知情的社會人士謊稱是觀世音菩薩轉世來人間。觀世音菩薩乃是　正法明如來倒駕慈航來當等覺大士，不可能連實證初果的智慧都沒有，更不可能至今還不能開悟，所以否定開悟明心的標的如來藏心，凡是沒有悟得如來藏心的人都是不明白法界實相智慧的人；由此可見那些擴大渲染達賴喇嘛是觀世音菩薩轉世之說法，純粹是政教合一的愚民手段而已；只有愚癡迷信的人，才會相信達賴喇嘛是觀世音菩薩轉世的說法。而且這些喇嘛教的上師、喇嘛們所說的相似佛法，只是假借佛法的名相，實質內涵卻是朝向精修無上瑜伽樂空雙運的邪淫法，本質上是閨房中的男女性交技藝，根本就與佛法無關；但是這些喇嘛們卻套用佛經中的名詞，如此穿鑿附會的欺瞞眾生。這樣公然撒謊欺騙民眾，有智慧的台灣人民是不能接受的，只有迷信而愚癡的人才會盲目信受；也只有已經與喇嘛上過床的女性，或者已經犯下邪淫戒的出家人，才會繼續支持喇嘛教。

　　台灣地區一切有智慧的人，都應該拒絕達賴所帶領的喇嘛徒眾大肆搜刮台灣人民的血汗錢；也應該拒絕喇嘛教繼續玷污台灣佛教中原本清淨的出家人，更應該拒絕喇嘛誘拐您的妻女合修雙身法。聰明的台灣男人，應該拒絕喇嘛誘拐或性侵台灣的女人；所有台灣的男人都應該齊心合力，共同預防被喇嘛暗中戴上綠帽子。您如果毫無警覺的讓妻子修習密宗—喇嘛教—的結果，您的妻子是遲早都

Despite the factual evidence presented, the Dalai Lama, who is just an ordinary person, still shamelessly allows his followers to lie to the ignorant public that he is the reincarnation of Bodhisattva Avalokitesvara. In fact, Bodhisattva Avalokitesvara is the True Dharma Enlightenment Tathagata, who became the equal-enlightenment bodhisattva in reverse order; it is impossible for him not to attain the wisdom of realizing the first fruit, and even more impossible for him not to get enlightened. Since getting enlightened means having found the Tathagatagarbha mind, the Dalai Lama denying the existence of Tathagatagarbha reflects the fact that he does not get enlightened yet. Those who do not get enlightened are ignorant of the true reality in the dharma world. Consequently, the greatly exaggerated claims about the Dalai Lama being the reincarnation of Bodhisattva Avalokitesvara are merely the deliberate manipulation through political and religious power to fool people. Only those foolish, superstitious people will believe that the Dalai Lama is the reincarnation of Bodhisattva Avalokitesvara. The fake Buddha dharma that the Lamaistic gurus (teachers) and lamas talk about is only using the Buddhist terms but with the essential contents of practicing the obscene Dual Operations of Bliss and Emptiness of the Highest Yoga Tantra. Essentially, it is the skill of copulation between male and female and has completely nothing to do with the Buddha dharma. However, these lamas cheat the public by using the Buddhist terms and hiding the real contents of Tantric practice. The wise Taiwanese people will not accept the lamas' public lies; only those stupid, superstitious persons will believe them; and only those females who have made love with the lama or those monastic practitioners who have violated the precept of celibacy will continue to support Lamaism.

All the wise in Taiwan should refuse the lamas, led by the Dalai Lama, to widely take the huge money of Taiwanese people away, refuse Lamaism to continue defiling the monastic practitioners, who were clean and pure originally, and even refuse the lamas to seduce your wife or daughter for cultivating the Couple-Practice Tantra. The wise Taiwanese men should refuse the lamas to seduce or rape the Taiwanese females and prevent themselves from being cuckolded by the lamas in secret. If you allow your wife to cultivate the Tantric practice, sooner or later, it will result in the secret co-practice of the Couple-Practice Tantra of copulation between your wife and the lama because it is the root doctrine of Lamaism. Unfortunately, this is the current situation—the males, whose wives cultivate Tantric Lamaism, have been cuckolded. Those Taiwanese men not only let their wives have sex with the lamas or living-buddhas in secret for the Dual Operation of

要與喇嘛暗中上床合修雙身法的,因為雙身法本來就是密宗─喇嘛教─的根本教義。戴著這頂特大號的綠帽子,居然是台灣所有修習藏傳「佛教」─密宗喇嘛教─女信徒們的丈夫的現況。台灣男人不僅讓妻子暗地裡與喇嘛、活佛們上床合修無上瑜伽樂空雙運,而且還要高高興興的讓妻子把自己辛苦賺來的錢財,供養這些喇嘛、活佛們;這其實是把自己的辛苦錢,經由妻子去向喇嘛買來大綠帽,再由妻子暗中為自己戴了綠帽,而喇嘛們依舊繼續公開在台灣大搖大擺地接受禮拜與供養,暗中則是繼續在房間裡與台灣男人的妻子上床合修雙身法,這是何等可悲的事情。

這次八八風災達賴喇嘛又想藉機來台灣大撈一票,美其名說是為台灣百姓祈福,想要展現他們「博愛」的一面,但是台灣民眾卻不知道他們「博愛」的本質就是要與一切女人性交,要使所有女人都獲得性愛的快樂,就是想要與咱們的台灣女性擴大交合,美其名為修行無上瑜伽。而且我們應該探討一個事實:達賴喇嘛向 佛陀祈福有效嗎?我們隨後將在此書中加以探討。因此對於達賴喇嘛派遣大量喇嘛們來到台灣,以種種假借佛教的名義而性侵善良學佛女性的惡形真相,我們不能坐視不管,不能任由台灣的女性被這些喇嘛們染指而失去貞操,所以我們站出來呼籲:**達賴喇嘛乃是自始至終都鼓勵性交雙身法,不管他們如何假借「佛法名詞」來美化矯飾,都與佛法無關。達賴喇嘛的修行,遠遠不如台灣本土持戒清淨的任何一位出家人;並且是嚴重毀犯了 佛陀清淨禁戒,是已經造下阿鼻地獄重罪的惡人;依據佛戒,死後必下地獄。並且達賴是以外道法取代 釋迦牟尼佛的正法,也是徹底破壞佛教正法的惡人,諸佛都厭惡這種人;既然如此,不管達賴的法會辦得再大、法器吹得多麼響,邪淫而且破壞正法的達賴喇嘛之祈福,當然不會獲得諸佛菩薩的支持,他的祈福當然是無效的!**

Happiness and Emptiness of the Highest Yoga Tantra but also happily let their wives offer the money, which they earn hard, to the lamas or living-buddhas. These lamas continue to receive the worship and offerings in public, but continue to have sex with the Taiwanese men's wives for the Couple-Practice Tantra in private. What a pitiful thing!

Again, the Dalai Lama took the chance of the typhoon disaster on August 8 and came to Taiwan to earn huge money, under the dignified name of his prayer for Taiwanese people. It seems they want to show their "love for all" to Taiwanese people, but Taiwanese people do not know that the substance of their "love for all" is to have sex with all women and make them get the sexual happiness. It means they want to extensively make love with all Taiwanese females, but they dignify it in the name of cultivating the Highest Yoga Tantra. On the other hand, we should explore the following question: Is it effective that the Dalai Lama pray to the Buddha for blessing? Due to the visits of many lamas, which are assigned by the Dalai Lama, lots of sexual assaults on Taiwanese virtuous females occur under the guise of Buddhism. We cannot just let it happens without any action; we cannot bear that Taiwanese females are defiled by the lamas and lose their chastity. Therefore, we stand out and advocate:

The Dalai Lama encourages the cultivation of the Couple-Practice Tantra all the time. Regardless how much effort they use to dignify the Tantric practice with the "Buddhist terms," it has completely nothing to do with the Buddha dharma. The Dalai Lama's practice attainment is far below that of any local Taiwanese monastic practitioner who cleanly and purely keeps his precept. In addition, the Dalai Lama has seriously violated the Buddha's clean, pure precept and is the evil person who has committed the gross sin of the Avici Hell; according to the Buddhist precept, he will definitely fall down to the hell after death. The Dalai Lama is the evil one who replaces Buddha Sakyamuni's dharma with the non-Buddhist dharma and completely destroys the Buddhist true dharma. Since all Buddhas dislike this kind of persons, the prayer of the Dalai Lama, who commits sexual misconduct as well as damages the true dharma, will not be supported by all Buddhas no matter how big the ceremony is or how loud the sounds of Buddhist musical instruments are. Therefore, his prayer is useless!

We not only identify in public that what the Dalai Lama does is damaging the

　　我們在此公開指出達賴所作所爲是破壞正法，也要勸達賴喇嘛公開聲明：**揚棄雙身法，並將法會的所得全數捐給台灣苦難的災民！**

　　正覺教育基金會的許多會員，這次爲了要揭露藏傳「佛教」邪淫雙身法的底細，爲了加強保護台灣女性免被無端染指，也爲了避免台灣男人被喇嘛們暗中戴上了綠帽子，因此在達賴喇嘛假借祈福名義來台撈錢之時，有四百人自動自發一起去高雄抗議，藉此機會教育台灣民眾，及早遠離密宗而不再受害。本書就彙整一些新聞報導刊載，並在後面舉證辨正藏傳「佛教」雙身法的內涵，而且長期持續流通，以教化百姓，讓大家都不會受騙；也籲請有智慧的台灣人，應爲台灣多做好事、不要再危害台灣於無形，去支持誘姦或性侵女性的喇嘛教。因爲引請外來的仿冒佛教的假修行者─喇嘛或活佛─來作表面功夫，其實是引狼入室，是使本來清淨的台灣，變成到處都有邪淫惡業的國土，同時也招來假冒佛菩薩的山精鬼魅，果報是未來的天災將會比這次八八水災還要嚴重。聰明的台灣人，不要戒行不清淨而提倡雙身法邪淫、與女徒弟輪座雜交的達賴喇嘛來祈福，也不要教導大家邪淫的達賴喇嘛爲台灣佛教徒灌頂說法。我們需要的是有清淨戒行的佛教法師來爲台灣祈福。如今台灣密宗如此氾濫，凡是家中妻子正在修學密宗的台灣男性，都已生活在**綠帽疑雲**之中：您學密的妻子與喇嘛上過床了嗎？您的頭頂很可能已被喇嘛們暗中戴上綠帽了。

true dharma but also advise him to proclaim in public: **to abandon the Couple-Practice Tantra and donate all the income of this ceremony to the suffering Taiwanese people!**

This time, while the Dalai Lama visited Taiwan to collect money in the name of prayer for blessings, around four hundred bodhisattvas of the True Enlightenment Education Foundation automatically stood out and went to Kaohsiung to protest against him with the purposes of disclosing the obscene fact of the Couple-Practice Tantra in Tibetan "Buddhism," extensively protecting the Taiwanese females from being defiled, preventing the Taiwanese males from being cuckolded in secret by the lamas, and educating Taiwanese people to keep far away from the Tantric Lamaism as sooner as possible so that they would not be harmed. We summarize the related media reports in this book, identifies the contents of the Couple-Practice Tantra in the later part of the book with evidence, and distributes it continuously so as to educate the public to avoid being cheated. We also appeal to the wise Taiwanese people to do more good things, not supporting the lamas, who seduce or rape the Taiwanese females, so that the lamas will no longer hurt Taiwan in a hidden way. Inviting the foreign lamas or living-buddhas, who disguise themselves as the Buddhist practitioners, is in fact to set a fox to keep one's geese and make this land, which is clean and pure originally, have obscene evil karma everywhere. It also attracts the ghosts and demons, who disguise themselves as the Buddhas or bodhisattvas, and results in more severe disasters than this one in the future. The wise should refuse the prayers, empowerments, and teachings of the Dalai Lama, who promotes the evil couple-practice of copulation with multiple female followers and does not hold the pure precepts. What we need is the prayer from the true Buddhist dharma-masters with clean, pure precept. With the Tantric practice flooding in Taiwan now, those males whose wives are Tantric learners will possibly be **cuckolded** and should have the following questions: Does my wife have sex with the lama? Am I cuckolded by the lama in secret?

密宗喇嘛寺院雙身像揭密：

Disclosing the secret about the couple-body statues in the Tantric temples of Lamaism:

中國大陸西安廣仁寺供奉喇嘛教的男女雙身像，一般時間蓋上遮羞布來遮掩其
修雙身法的狀況（左圖）與取下遮羞布後顯見其修雙身法的實況（右圖）。
2009/12/3、2010/4/8 拍攝。

2010/04/08 15:40

These are the couple-body statues of Lamaism worshipped in Guangren Temple, Xian, China. Usually, the lower part of each statue is veiled to cover up their involvement in the couple-practice of copulation (left photo); when the veil is removed, it shows clearly the fact of the couple-practice of copulation (right photo). Photograph taken on December 3, 2009 and April 8, 2010 respectively.

阎罗法王

中國瀋陽的喇嘛教寺院——北塔護國法輪寺，其所弘揚的就是密宗無上瑜伽男女性交的雙身像。拍攝日期：2009/12/13。

The couple-body statue in a Lamaistic temple, North Pagoda Huguo Dharma Wheel Temple, Shengyang, China. They propagate the Tantric couple-practice copulation of the Highest Yoga Tantra. Photograph taken on December 13, 2009.

沈阳北塔护国法轮寺
2009-12-13 14:25

請冷靜的理解：您的老婆或家中女性若與密宗喇嘛、活佛們修學佛法，最後一定要這樣「無上瑜伽」——交合起來。

Just think calmly: Eventually, your wife or other female family members will cultivate the couple-practice of copulation of "the Highest Yoga Tantra" with the Tantric gurus or living-buddhas like this.

沈阳北塔护国法轮寺
2009-12-13 14:24

不論喇嘛們宣稱的是「無上瑜伽、大樂光明、大手印、大圓滿、樂空雙運」
等，都是要與美貌女信徒一一性交的雙身法。

Whatever the lamas call it, "the Highest Yoga Tantra, radiance of bliss, Mahamudra, Great
Perfection, Dual Operations of Bliss and Emptiness, etc.," they all refer to the couple-practice of
copulation, which means to copulate with beautiful female followers in turn.

許多信受或修學藏傳「佛教」的寺院中，都暗中供奉喇嘛教的雙身像；因為以達賴為首的藏傳「佛教」本質是源自印度性力派的生殖崇拜而冒用佛法，他們高唱博愛，是要與天下所有女人性交，達到「樂空雙運」，「博愛」只是謀取免費淫樂的藉口。

Actually, the Lamaistic couple-body statues are hidden in many temples of Tibetan "Buddhism." Why is that? It is because Tibetan "Buddhism," led by the Dalai Lama, essentially comes from the Hindu Tantrism, which worships sex and reproduction, in the guise of Buddhism. They promote "love for all" for the purpose of copulating with all women in the world and achieving "the Dual Operations of Bliss and Emptiness." In fact, "love for all" is just an excuse to have sexual pleasure for free.

沈陽北塔護國法輪寺
2009-12-13 14:21

瀋陽北塔護國法輪寺的坐姿男女雙身像。2009/12/13 拍攝。

The couple-body statue in sitting posture in North Pagoda Huguo Dharma Wheel Temple, Shengyang, China. Photograph taken on December 13, 2009.

沈阳北塔护国
2009-12-13

沈阳北塔护国法轮寺
2009-12-13 14:26

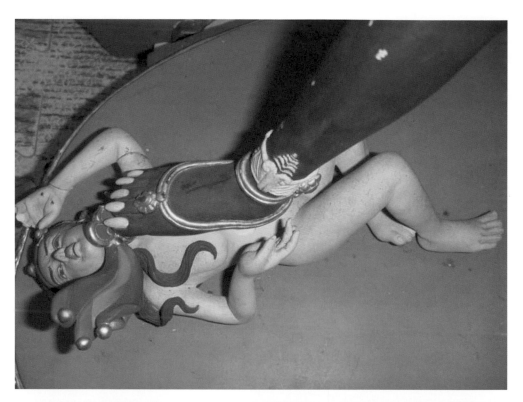

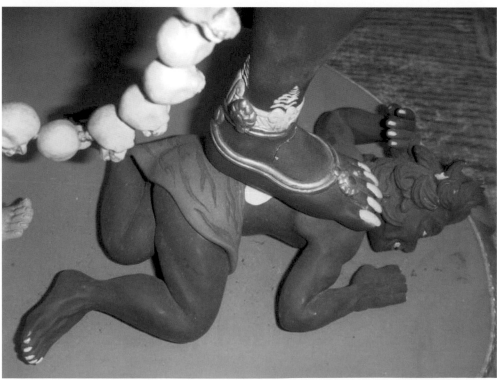

修雙身法的
喇嘛教
不是佛教！

Lamaism,

with the Couple-Practice Tantra,

is not Buddhism!

一、達賴喇嘛的祈福是無效的

以達賴為首的藏傳「佛教」—喇嘛教—想用「雙身法無上瑜伽性交」的方法，來廣行「博愛」——愛盡天下的女人；透過這次台灣八八水災來祈福的名義，想要擴大密宗在台灣的勢力，想要在未來從台灣撈得更多錢財，擴大密宗流亡政府更大的財源。但達賴的祈福是絕對無效的，我們可以從很多的層面舉出論證，證明**達賴喇嘛的祈福乃是無效的**：

一者、藏傳「佛教」常常宣傳達賴喇嘛為觀世音菩薩轉世，而且達賴喇嘛已經號稱轉世十四次了，現任的達賴喇嘛為第十四世；但是我們從可稽的歷史資料及事實來看，歷代達賴喇嘛絕大多數都是未成年即夭折死亡，短命早夭的多，甚至很多世都是不到二十歲就夭折死亡。由這個簡單的事實現象，就可以知道達賴喇嘛根本就不是觀世音菩薩轉世，他只是一介凡夫而已，卻被政教合一的愚民政策及宣傳，吹捧為大菩薩轉世；如今又藉政治運作前來台灣，謊稱是來為台灣人民祈福灌頂。而這個主張廣修雙身法的邪淫宗教首領，根本沒有資格也沒有能力祈福，所以他向諸佛菩薩祈福絕對是無效的。因為有佛法知見的人都知道，觀世音菩薩乃是倒駕慈航福慧圓滿的等覺大菩薩，不可能有年幼夭折的事情發生；只有藏傳「佛教」中才有短命夭壽的「活佛」，正統佛教中沒有這樣短命的佛菩薩。若有藏密人士辯說：「這些夭折的歷代達賴喇嘛乃是被政治鬥爭迫害殺死的。」這樣的說法更能反應達賴喇嘛不是觀世音菩薩的化身與轉世，因為觀世音菩薩乃是過去 正法明如來倒駕慈航，本來就已經成佛；由於大慈大悲的緣故而示現為等覺大士，來救護苦難眾生；而且諸佛乃是福德具足、智慧具足的兩足尊，豈會如此沒有福報而有夭折短命早死的情形發生？那怎麼能夠稱為福德具

I Dalai Lama's Prayer Being Useless

Tibetan "Buddhism," led by the Dalai Lama, or called Lamaism, tries to use the "copulation of the Couple-Practice Tantra of the Highest Yoga Tantra" to have "love for all"—loving all women in the world. In the name of praying for the victims of the typhoon disaster, they want to expand their power in Taiwan, get more money from Taiwan, and enlarge the financial resources of Tibetan exiled government. But in fact, the **Dalai Lama's prayer is useless**. We can prove it through the three arguments as follows:

First, Tibetan "Buddhism" usually exaggerates that the Dalai Lama is the reincarnation of Bodhisattva Avalokitesvara and have been reincarnated for fourteen times till now; the current Dalai Lama is the fourteenth generation. However, from the recorded historical data, we can find that most of the Dalai Lamas in the history died before they became an adult, many of them being dead before twenty years old. From this simple fact, we can conclude that the Dalai Lama is by no means the reincarnation of Bodhisattva Avalokitesvara but an ordinary person, who is exaggerated as the great bodhisattva through the governmental religious policy of fooling people and media promotion. This time, through the political manipulation, he came to Taiwan in the name of prayer and empowerment. Because of promoting the extensive cultivation of the Couple-Practice Tantra, he does not have the qualification and capability to pray for people, and thus his prayer to Buddhas or bodhisattvas is definitely useless. Those who have Buddhist knowledge all know that Bodhisattva Avalokitesvara is the great bodhisattva of equal-enlightenment who has perfected the virtuous welfare and supra-mundane wisdom; it is impossible for her to die so young. Only in Tibetan "Buddhism" but not in the true Buddhism, there exists the "living-buddhas" who died in their early age. If someone argues: "These Dalai Lamas who died early is because of political conflict and oppression," this kind of talk can even prove the Dalai Lama is not the reincarnation of Bodhisattva Avalokitesvara since Bodhisattva Avalokitesvara had been the True Dharma Enlightenment Tathagata, who became the bodhisattva in reverse order, and had been a Buddha already; due to the great kindness and compassion, Bodhisattva Avalokitesvara manifests herself as the equal-enlightenment bodhisattva to rescue the suffering sentient beings. All Buddhas have perfected their virtuous welfare and wisdom, it is impossible for them to die so early, without the worldly welfare at all. It is even more impossible for them to die by the political oppression. Those who die by the political

足圓滿的無上正等正覺的佛陀呢？豈有被政治迫害而死的佛！若有的話，那就不是真正的佛。但是藏傳「佛教」的法王活佛—歷代達賴喇嘛—卻是夭折而死的多，而且是多次轉世都夭折而死；所以「歷代短命的達賴喇嘛是觀世音菩薩轉世」的謊言，只能迷惑無智慧而迷信之人；而且只有「藏傳佛教——喇嘛教」中才有「夭折佛」的情形發生，唯有迷信者才會相信喇嘛教這樣的說法，有理性、有智慧者是不會相信的。因此這個假冒為佛的達賴喇嘛，他來台灣所作的祈福根本無效，他只是假借宗教的名義在搞「西藏獨立」的政治活動，也是前來支持台灣暗中勾引婦女修雙身法的密宗而已。因此大家應該要認清一個事實：**達賴喇嘛只是一個政客、假修行人，一個二六時中都想與女人修雙身法的凡夫而已。**

　　二者、若從佛法的角度來看，達賴喇嘛乃是以**意識心永恆不滅**的常見外道法來取代佛教正法，也是以一心專注於男女交合中的淫樂—無上瑜伽樂空雙運—說為無上修行證量，這根本不是清淨的佛教徒，所以這樣犯戒邪淫的人，他向諸佛菩薩祈福是絕對無效的。而且達賴喇嘛這次來台，乃是因為他想透過台灣八八水災的災民，假借祈福之名義來作「藏獨」的政治秀；同時來斂財——廣收供養，以及推廣喇嘛教的「博愛」（無上瑜伽——愛盡天下女人）的性交雙身法而已；這樣邪淫的人所辦的祈福，根本沒有祈福的功效，可憐的是甚多無智迷信的人，仍然願意盲從追隨之。

　　三者、號稱「藏傳佛教」最高法王的達賴喇嘛，也是否定 釋迦牟尼佛正法的破法者，他這樣毀謗 釋迦牟尼佛：

> 根據一般大乘佛教的觀念，佛陀有三次重要的轉法輪—傳統上，佛陀對弟子主要的三次佛法教示，傳統上稱為三轉法輪。嚴格的說，這三次轉法輪所開示的法教是互相矛盾

oppression will not be the true Buddha. However in Tibetan "Buddhism," the living-buddhas, the Dalai Lamas of many generations, mostly died early, with the incarnations of very short life. Consequently, the lie that "the Dalai Lama is the reincarnation of Bodhisattva Avalokitesvara" can only confuse those who lack wisdom and are superstitious; only in Tibetan "Buddhism," Lamaism, there exists the short-life-buddha, and only those superstitious persons will believe this claim of Lamaism; the prayers of this Dalai Lama, who disguises himself as a Buddha, are completely in vain; he engages in the political activities of "Tibet independence" in the name of religion and came to Taiwan for supporting lamas, who seduces the females to cultivate the Couple-Practice Tantra in secret. Therefore, we should recognize the following fact: **The Dalai Lama is only a politico, a fake practitioner and an ordinary person who always intends to cultivate the Couple-Practice Tantra with females.**

Second, from the Buddhist viewpoint, the Dalai Lama replaces the true Buddha dharma with the non-Buddhist eternalism, **which thinks the conscious mind is permanent and never ceasing,** and regards the obscene happiness of concentrating on copulation, the Dual Operations of Bliss and Emptiness of the Highest Yoga Tantra, as the highest realization level of practice. With such behavior, he is never the clean, pure Buddhist. This person's prayer to the Buddhas and bodhisattvas is absolutely useless. In addition, the purposes of his visit to Taiwan this time are to make a political show of "Tibet independence" in the name of praying for the typhoon victims, to collect wealth through Taiwanese people's offering, and to propagate the Couple-Practice Tantra of the Highest Yoga Tantra in the name of Lamaistic "love for all"—loving all women in the whole world. The prayer ceremony held by this kind of person does not have any effect at all. But it is a pity that many stupid, superstitious persons are still willing to blindly follow him.

Third, the Dalai Lama, the so-called the highest dharma-king of "Tibetan Buddhism," is actually the dharma destroyer who negates the true dharma of Buddha Sakyamuni; he slanders the Buddha with the following statements:

> According to the general Mahayana point of view, there were three major turnings of the wheel, as the three main cycles of the Buddha's teachings are traditionally called. The teachings that were given during these three major turnings of the wheel are literally **contradictory**—some elements are really incompatible. (Jeremy Hayward and Francisco J. Varela, *Gentle Bridges: Conversations with the Dalai Lama on the Sciences of Mind,* 1992,

的—某些内容不相符合。（杰瑞米·海華、法蘭西斯可·瓦瑞拉 編著，靳文穎 譯，《揭開心智的奧秘》，1996/06/30 初版，眾生文化出版有限公司（台灣），頁 71。）

由此可知達賴喇嘛對於如來第三轉法輪的聖教乃是全然毀謗、否定的，也可知道達賴根本不信前後三轉法輪諸經的一致性；而我們經由實證以後，卻已經證明 釋迦如來前後三轉法輪所說的諸經中的教義，全都相符相契而沒有絲毫矛盾之處。由這裡也證明達賴根本不懂初轉法輪到第三轉法輪的所有經典教義，才會嚴重誤會而隨意毀謗；這已證明達賴全無實證三乘菩提，故無法了達三轉法輪諸經法義的一致性，才會認為三轉法輪經典的法教「**互相矛盾**」，像這樣的凡夫竟然自稱是觀世音菩薩轉世，也只有愚癡人才會相信。達賴主張 如來第二轉法輪的說法最為殊勝，卻貶斥第二轉法輪般若智慧根本的第八識如來藏，如其在書中說：

至於我的立場，則是駁斥根本識的存在。（達賴喇嘛著，楊書婷、姚怡平譯，《達賴：心與夢的解析》，2004/12 出版，四方書城有限公司，頁 83。）

這是因為達賴還沒有實證法界實相心，更不可能相信三轉法輪諸經中所說的聖教：一切眾生依據實證法界實相心阿賴耶識如來藏而轉依修行，最後可以成佛。所以才敢造下誹謗菩薩藏的大惡業，如此謗佛而造下破壞佛陀正法大惡業者，若請這種人來祈福當然無效。

四者、喇嘛們盜用佛教的名義，號稱藏傳「佛教」，而且謊稱男女性交雙身法——無上瑜伽樂空雙運灌頂是佛門中的修行方法；但是這種男女性交之法，乃是古印度性力派的外道法，只是原始宗教「生殖崇拜」的信徒而已，乃是典型的印度教中的末流所倡

Boston, Mass: Shambhala Publications, p.31)

From above cited passage, we can know the Dalai Lama slanders the Buddha and negates all the holy teachings of the Buddha's third turning of the wheel; he does not believe the consistency of the sutras in the three turnings of the wheel during different time periods. On the other hand, through the actual realization, we have proven the Buddha's doctrines in all sutras of the three turnings of the wheel in different times are completely consistent, without any conflict. It also proves that the Dalai Lama does not understand all the doctrines of the three turnings of the wheel. Therefore he seriously misunderstands them and arbitrarily makes the slander. From this, we can know that he has not yet actually realized the *bodhi* of three vehicles; thus he cannot master the consistency of the doctrines among all sutras of the three turnings and concludes they are **literally contradictory to each other**. Only the stupid persons will believe that such an ordinary person is the reincarnation of Bodhisattva Avalokitesvara. Although the Dalai Lama claims the teaching of the second turning is the best, he devalues the eighth *vijnana* [discernment], Tathagatagarbha, which is the root of *prajna* wisdom in the second turning. For example, he says in his book:

> As far as my own position is concerned, I totally refute the existence of the foundation consciousness. (Francisco J. Varela, *Sleeping, Dreaming and Dying,* 1997, Boston: Wisdom Publications, p.87)

Since the Dalai Lama has not yet actually realized the true mind of the dharma-realm, it is impossible for him to believe the holy teaching of the sutras in the three turnings: If all sentient beings can actually realize the true mind, the Alaya *vijnana* Tathagatagarbha, and practice accordingly, they can become Buddhas finally. Since he has not yet found it, he dares to commit such a grave evil karma of slandering the holy teaching. If one invites this kind of person, who slanders the Buddha and commits the serious evil karma of destroying the true dharma, for prayer, it is obviously in vain.

Fourth, the lamas steal the Buddhist terms, claim their practice as Tibetan "Buddhism," and lie that the Couple-Practice Tantra of copulation—the empowerment with the Dual Operations of Bliss and Emptiness in the Highest Yoga Tantra—is a Buddhist practice method. Nevertheless, this kind of copulation method by a male and female couple is in fact a non-Buddhist practice of Tantrism in ancient India, nothing but a "Procreation Worship" of primitive religion; it is

導的性力派思想；而這種樂空雙運—大樂光明—無上瑜伽，所追求
的第一喜（男女根的長久樂觸）到第四喜（從男女根擴大到全身的長久樂
觸——密宗的抱身佛境界），既與阿羅漢所證解脫道的斷我見、我執無
關，也與佛菩提道菩薩所證悟的見道（明心見性）完全無關；所以「藏
傳佛教——喇嘛教」根本就不是佛門弟子，因此他們只是不信清淨
佛法，卻假冒「佛教」名義的凡夫。這些證據已經證明一件事實：
這些人是無根據地毀謗佛菩薩者，也是破壞佛教正法教義者，又是
造下極多邪淫惡業而大量損福的人，所信奉的也是山精鬼魅化現的
假佛菩薩；若邀請他們來祈福，即是邀請山精鬼魅前來台灣而暗中
帶來天災的種子；也是請諸佛菩薩所不喜愛的謗佛破法者來祈福，
能不能達成祈福的目的？有智慧的您，稍微想一下就知道了！所以
花大錢邀請達賴
來台灣祈福，遠
不如邀請台灣本
土清淨修行的法
師們來祈福更有
效。所以在實際
上，達賴等人的
祈福根本無效。

exactly the Tantric thought that was promoted at the ending age of Hinduism. All states of the Dual Operations of Bliss and Emptiness in the Highest Yoga Tantra, from the first joy (the long tactile happiness of both male and female sexual organs) to the fourth joy (the long tactile happiness extended from the sexual organ to the whole body—the state of Tantric reward-body buddha), have completely nothing to do with the eliminations of self-view and self-attachment, which are the *arhats'* realization of the Liberation-Way, and also have nothing to do with seeing the Way (getting enlightened or seeing the Buddha-nature), which is actually realized by the bodhisattvas of the Buddhahood-Way. Consequently "Tibetan Buddhism" is by no means Buddhism; they are the ordinary people who do not believe in the clean, pure Buddha dharma and steal the name of "Buddhism." The evidence can also prove a fact: The lamas groundlessly slander the Buddhas and bodhisattvas, destroy the true Buddhist doctrines, commit huge evil karmas of sexual misconduct, and have lost lots of welfare; since they believe in the fake buddha and bodhisattvas disguised by ghosts or demons, inviting them for blessing is the same as inviting the ghosts and demons to Taiwan, bringing the seeds of future natural disaster in secret; this

invitation also means to invite the person whom the Buddha and bodhisattvas dislike for prayer; can it achieve the purpose of blessing? The wise like you can know the answer easily. Therefore, spending huge money to invite the Dalai Lama to Taiwan for prayer is far more ineffective than to invite native Taiwanese dharma masters who have clean, pure practice for prayer. In fact, nothing can be obtained from the prayer of the Dalai Lama and his followers.

各地密宗喇嘛性醜聞，法王、喇嘛、活佛們就是這樣與所有美麗年輕的女信徒性交，美其名爲雙修樂空雙運。

The sex scandals about the Tantric lamas happen in many different places. The dharma-kings, *lamas*, or living-buddhas, have copulation with all the beautiful young female believers like this. They dignify it with the name of couple practicing the Dual Operations of Bliss and Emptiness.

二、達賴喇嘛不是一位和平者

密宗喇嘛們長期而廣泛蹂躪婦女、女童，騙財、騙色！達賴喇嘛自己也在書中坦白的說：

> 對於佛教徒來說，倘若修行者有著堅定的智慧和慈悲，則可以**運用性交在修行的道上**，因為這可以引發意識的強大專注力，目的是為了要彰顯與延長心更深刻的層面（稍早有關死亡過程時曾描述）為的是要把力量用在強化空性領悟上。否則僅僅只是性交，與心靈修行完全無關。當一個人在動機和智慧上的修行已經達到很高的階段，那麼就算是**兩性相交或一般所謂的性交**，也不會減損這個人的純淨行為。在修行道上已達到很高程度的瑜伽行者，是完全有資格進行雙修，而具有這樣能力的出家人是可以維持住他的戒律。（達賴喇嘛著，《修行的第一堂課》，2002年初版，先覺出版股份有限公司，頁 177-178。）

事實上，性交永遠不可能是佛法修行的工具，卻是藏傳「佛教」—喇嘛教—假冒佛教盡情縱慾的藉口；因為即使是佛法中基礎的禪定都必須遠離淫慾才能證得，阿羅漢與菩薩、諸佛的修證也都必須斷除淫慾而超越欲界的，所以佛法三乘菩提中一向都否定性交的，因為這只是意識境界，與常見外道相同。只有無知於真實佛法之人，才會誑言性交也是佛法；達賴喇嘛這樣說，只是要使喇嘛們合法地淫人妻女而已；只有迷信達賴大名聲的無智者，才會誤信而攀緣加持、祈福、追隨，而妄想透過性交成佛。事實上，無上瑜伽雙修法只是達賴喇嘛等藏傳「佛教」的師徒們，貪求淫行的詭辯藉口與欺瞞托詞。因為真正佛教中的出家人乃是

II   Dalai Lama Never a Messenger of Peace

The lamas of Tibetan Buddhism have been sexually abusing many women and girls for a long time; they collect money by fraud and are love swindlers. In his book, the Dalai Lama frankly says:

> For Buddhists, **sexual intercourse can be used** in the spiritual path because it causes a strong focusing of consciousness if the practitioner has firm compassion and wisdom. Its purpose is to manifest and prolong the deeper levels of mind (described earlier with respect to the process of dying), in order to put their power to use in strengthening the realization of emptiness. Otherwise, mere intercourse has nothing to do with spiritual cultivation. When a person has achieved a high level of practice in motivation and wisdom, then even **the joining of the two sex organs, or so-called intercourse**, does not detract from the maintenance of that person's pure behavior. Yogis who have achieved a high level of the path and are fully qualified can engage in sexual activity and a monastic with this ability can maintain all the precepts. (Dalai Lama XIV/translated and edited by Jeffrey Hopkins, *How to Practice: The Way to a Meaningful Life,* Pocket Books, a division of Simon & Schuster, Inc. NY, 2002, p.193.)

In fact, sexual intercourse can never be the means of Buddhist practice because one should be away from the sexual desire in order to attain even the basic *samadhi* in Buddhism. However, Tibetan "Buddhism" (or called Lamaism, a fake Buddhism) uses it as an excuse for indulging in the sensual pleasures. The practice of all *arhats*, bodhisattvas and Buddhas needs to eliminate the sexual desire so that they can transcend the desire-realm. Therefore, in the three-vehicle *bodhi* of Buddhism, sexual intercourse is always disapproved because it is only a state of the mind-*vijnana*, which is equivalent to the state of the non-Buddhist eternalism. Only those who are ignorant of the real Buddhism will brag that sexual intercourse is also a Buddhist dharma. Such a statement from the Dalai Lama is only to make the lamas rightfully have sex with other people's wives or daughters. Only those ignorant people who have blind faith in the famous Dalai Lama will cling to the lamas' blessings and wrongly believe that one can attain Buddhahood through sexual intercourse. In fact, for those gurus of the Tibetan "Buddhism," including the Dalai Lama, the Couple-Practice Tantra of the Highest Yoga Tantra (Anuttara-Yoga-Tantra) is only a deceptive excuse for their licentious behavior. The real Buddhist monastics take the precept of celibacy; one must be away from the greed for sexual

戒淫的，必須遠離性愛的貪著，身心清淨，才會產生禪定功德；更何況達賴喇嘛爲首的藏傳「佛教」——喇嘛教，所弘揚的乃是欲界最低等的邪淫—不顧人倫的邪淫—根本是使自己的未來世與信眾的未來世，都會與畜生道、地獄道相應的行爲，絕對不是佛教的修行法門。

藏密喇嘛多年來一直在台灣斂財，騙取台灣的資源、錢財，現在又假借台灣的苦難—八八水災—來台灣發災難財了。正當台灣災民受風災、水災而嚴重急需救濟時，達賴喇嘛假借祈福的名義來台灣斂財及作秀；**因此我們正覺教育基金會的會員公開聲明要求達賴喇嘛：「達賴喇嘛應把法會的收入全部轉爲救濟災民使用，在台灣災民正需要資源時，不要假借來台祈福帶走台灣人的善心與血汗錢。」**

有智慧又聰明的台灣人！請您冷靜的想一想：您還要將您的錢財捐獻給每年在台灣時時刻刻淫人妻女的喇嘛教嗎？還要找那些公開及私下專門修雙身法的無福人前來祈福嗎？其實台灣人民的人飢己飢、人溺己溺的互助精神，才是台灣的至寶，我們不要外來的騙徒作無效且招惡的儀式！達賴喇嘛的祈福，所招來的鬼神乃是護持鼓吹「藏傳佛教無上瑜伽的雙身法」的山精鬼魅，這樣祈福的結果會讓台灣與邪神淫鬼感應，也會使台灣的女人被喇嘛上師繼續邪淫，更讓台灣家中有女眷信仰藏傳「佛教」的男人，全都有著被偷戴綠帽的危機。居然有人邀請這樣的人來祈福！眞是荒唐，因爲達賴喇嘛的祈福乃是全然無效的！

如今很多人不明正邪，還大力護持披著「佛教」名義又弘揚邪淫雙身法的達賴喇嘛；更可怕與可悲的是，許多人把專修雙身

love, with a pure body and mind, so that he can have the merits and virtues of *samadhi*. The Tibetan "Buddhism," Lamaism led by the Dalai Lama, preaches adultery, which is a state in the lowest grade of desire-realm. Adultery, which violates the human ethics, is actually a behavior that will lead to the animal or hell path in the future lives of one and his followers; it is absolutely not a method of Buddhist practice.

The lamas of Tibetan Buddhism have collected wealth illegally in Taiwan for many years; they have cheated the Taiwanese followers out of their resources and money. Again, they came to Taiwan for raising money by taking advantage of the disaster of Taiwan **(August 8 Flood Disaster or called Typhoon Morakot Disaster)**. While the Taiwanese people were suffering from the typhoon disaster and in urgent need of help, the Dalai Lama came to Taiwan for show and collected wealth under the guise of praying for the blessings. **Therefore, the members of the True Enlightenment Education Foundation made a public request: "The Dalai Lama should give all the money raised from the prayer meeting to those victims of the disaster. Do not take advantage of the kindness of Taiwanese people and take away their hard-earned money in the name of praying for the blessings while the victims are in need of help."**

The wise Taiwanese people! Just think calmly: Are you still willing to donate your money to the lamas who always have sex with other people's wives or daughters in Taiwan every year? Do you still want to invite those who openly or privately focus on the Couple-Practice Tantra to pray for the blessings? To have mutual sympathy and to help each other are actually the most valuable treasure of Taiwanese people. We do not need a foreign swindler to perform the religious ceremony, which is ineffective and will lead to the evil results. The Dalai Lama's prayer will invite the demons and ghosts that support "the Couple-Practice Tantra of the Highest Yoga Tantra in Tibetan Buddhism." Such a prayer will make the Taiwanese connect with the lecherous devils and make the Taiwanese women continue to commit adultery with the lamas. Therefore, all the husbands of those female believers of Tibetan "Buddhism" will be in danger of wearing a green hat. (The Chinese slang "wearing a green hat" means that someone's wife is unfaithful.) It is incredible that someone invited such a person to pray for the blessings. It is absolutely ridiculous because the Dalai Lama's prayer is totally ineffective.

Today, many people who are ignorant of right and evil still strongly support

法、背地裡一直在淫亂自己妻女的喇嘛教，視爲佛教中的一個支派，只因爲他們打著藏傳「佛教」的名義，就一味的無知信仰，完全不想了知佛教教義內涵與喇嘛教的教義內涵完全不同。甚至還有人大力爲喇嘛教宣傳，讓「藏傳佛教無上瑜伽樂空雙運」的邪淫雙身法在台灣廣大弘揚開來，在迷信達賴喇嘛者的大力宣傳下，這股迷信達賴喇嘛的勢力，將成爲台灣女性繼續被淫亂的推手；至於所有支持妻子信受喇嘛教而學密的台灣男人，就在妻子被暗中淫亂的事實中，爲自己戴上了綠帽子，當上了龜公而不自知。

從佛法的角度來說，這樣大力護持**藏傳「佛教」雙身法**的人，也不知自己已經犯下未來世墮落地獄、畜生道的共業；即使這一世地位顯赫，學問很高；即使目前名聲極大，外表展現出很溫良謙恭，都將因爲無知助長邪淫爲本的喇嘛教，而使得社會道德淪喪到無以救贖的地步；這樣支持「藏傳佛教雙身法」的人，乃是誤導百姓跟著受累。現在我們能做的就是對喇嘛教大聲說「不」，我們將持續告訴民眾事實的眞相，希望導正社會大眾的知見，讓大家認清楚藏傳「佛教」—喇嘛教—自始至終邪淫的本質，同時也祈求佛菩薩冥冥中加持台灣男人智慧增長，都能阻絕家中的妻子親近密宗，免於綠帽疑雲蓋頂的威脅。

請大家共同努力救護台灣人民吧！請讓更多的台灣人民智慧增長！

祈願台灣的子民不再受到密宗上師、喇嘛、活佛的邪教導，誤以爲出家人可和女弟子邪淫合修雙身法。別讓「藏傳佛教」密宗雙身法繼續污染台灣，不再讓達賴喇嘛爲首的藏傳假佛教的喇

the Dalai Lama, who preaches the evil Couple-Practice Tantra under the guise of "Buddhism." It is even more terrible and miserable that many people wrongly consider Lamaism (its lamas focusing on the Couple-Practice Tantra and privately having sex with other people's wives or daughters) to be a branch school of Buddhism. They have blind faith in Tibetan "Buddhism" only because it is under the guise of Buddhism, and they do not want to know at all about the connotation of the Buddhist teachings, which is entirely different from that of Lamaism. Some people even strongly propagate Lamaism, making the evil Couple-Practice Tantra (the "Dual Operations of Bliss and Emptiness of the Highest Yoga Tantra in Tibetan Buddhism") widely spread in Taiwan. Under the influence of the strong propagation by those who have blind faith in the Dalai Lama, the Taiwanese females will continue to be sexually abused. As to those Taiwanese men who support their wives in learning Lamaism, they do not know that they are wearing a green hat after their wives have committed adultery secretly with the lamas.

From the Buddhist perspective, those who strongly support the **Couple-Practice Tantra of Tibetan "Buddhism"** also do not know that they have already created a collective karma that will lead to the hell and animal paths in their future lives. Even if one is in high social status or knowledgeable in this lifetime, or one is famous or outwardly modest at present, he will make the social morality decline to an extent that cannot be saved because he helps to spread the evil and licentious Lamaism due to ignorance. Those who support the "Couple-Practice Tantra of Tibetan Buddhism" are misleading the general people and get them into trouble. What we can do now is to say "No" to Lamaism. We will continue to tell people the true facts and hope to correct the knowledge of the public so that everyone can clearly understand the essence of Tibetan "Buddhism" (Lamaism), which is evil and licentious all the way. Let us pray that the Taiwanese men can increase their wisdom by the unseen help of Buddhas and bodhisattvas; they can keep their wives away from Tibetan Buddhism so that they are not in the danger of wearing a green hat.

Let us work together to help and protect the Taiwanese people and make their wisdom grow!

We pray that the Taiwanese people will not again receive the evil teachings of those Tantric gurus, lamas or living-buddhas and do not wrongly think that the Buddhist monks can have the couple-practice of copulation with the female

嘛們，繼續欺瞞台灣男人而與台灣男人的妻子們繼續邪淫；不再使無辜的台灣男人，因無知而讓妻子學密，以免暗中被喇嘛戴上了綠帽子；也不再讓喇嘛教假借佛教的名義，混在佛門中繼續欺矇迷信無知的出家人誤犯邪淫戒。我們期望台灣佛教界摒除邪淫的雙身法而清淨了，當台灣不再縱容女性被藏傳假佛教的喇嘛們蹂躪時，才能使台灣遠離喇嘛大量邪淫後製造出來的惡業種子繼續增長；唯有如此，才能使台灣遠離喇嘛們引來的假冒佛菩薩的山精鬼魅，在暗中共同引來天災。我們大聲呼籲：勇敢有智的台灣人民，應該自己來祈福，而不是由淫人妻女造下邪淫惡業的，而且是不受諸佛菩薩喜歡的達賴喇嘛來祈福。

試想：如果您的妻子與喇嘛暗地裡如此圖一樣合修雙身法——無上瑜伽，您難道不是綠帽罩頂的丈夫嗎？支持妻子追隨達賴喇嘛「藏傳佛教」修行，最後必然會是這樣的結果。

disciples. Do not let the Couple-Practice Tantra of "Tibetan Buddhism" continue to defile Taiwan. Do not let the lamas of the Tibetan fake Buddhism, led by the Dalai Lama, continue to deceive the Taiwanese men and to commit adultery with their female followers. The innocent Taiwanese men should not allow their wives to learn the Tantric practice lest they might wear a green hat. Do not let the *lamas* continue to deceive the ignorant, superstitious monastics into violating the precept of celibacy under the guise of Buddhism. We hope that the Buddhist world of Taiwan renounce the evil Couple-Practice Tantra and become pure. When the Taiwanese people can stop the lamas of Tibetan fake Buddhism from sexually abusing the females, the seeds of evil karma created by the lamas' adultery will stop to grow. Only this way can Taiwan be away from the natural disasters induced secretly by the demons and ghosts, which are the fake buddhas and bodhisattvas invited by the lamas. We make a serious public request: The brave and wise Taiwanese! The prayer ceremony should be performed by us but not by the Dalai Lama, who creates the evil karma of adultery and is not welcomed by all Buddhas and bodhisattvas.

Just think: If your wife has the couple-practice of copulation (the Highest Yoga Tantra) with a lama as shown in this picture, aren't you wearing a green hat? Anyone who supports his wife to practice the teachings of "Tibetan Buddhism," led by the Dalai Lama, will inevitably have this result.

三、邪教比天災還可怕

——密宗雙身法之真相

甲、密宗喇嘛努力修中脈、氣功，甚至勤練盤腿跳躍，這些都是為了要與女信徒合修雙身法而作準備：如同附圖一般抱著女信徒交合時跳躍，增強淫樂觸覺

藏密喇嘛號稱可以即身成佛，因此在實修雙身法前，會很努力的修中脈、氣功，如達賴喇嘛說：

> 入睡與死亡的經歷來自於體內不同元素的分解，這個分解過程會發生在許多不同的時候。例如，在特定的觀想禪修中，便會出現這種分解。這些元素的分解或解離，相應於不同粗細層次的心識。無論這種分解何時出現，都是由於體內氣的改變而出現不同粗細層次的心識。有三種方式可以讓身體的氣產生改變。第一種純粹是自然的生理過程，這是由於不同元素的分解，包括地大（堅固性）、水大（流動性）、火大（熱）、風大（動作性）。在睡眠與死亡的過程，這些會自然出現、無法控制。另一種類似的氣的改變是特定禪修的結果，主要透過專注與想像。這能讓心識從粗重轉到微細的層次，而產生氣的改變。第三種則是**透過性交行為**。不過，一般人的交媾無法達到這種能量的移動和心識粗細層次的改變。唯有透過特定的修持，**控制性交時生殖液的流動才有可能發生，男女皆然。**（達賴喇嘛著，楊書婷、姚怡平譯，《達賴：心與夢的解析》，2004 年 12 月出版，四方書城有限公司，頁 44。）

從達賴喇嘛這裡的說法，就很明確的顯示：喇嘛教努力勤練氣

III Evil Religion More Terrible than Natural Disaster —The true facts of the Couple-Practice Tantra in Tibetan Buddhism

1 Tantric lamas cultivating the central channel and Chi-Practice, and even diligently practicing jumping in a cross-legged sitting posture for exercising the Couple-Practice Tantra with female followers

The lamas of Tibetan Buddhism claim that they can attain Buddhahood in this lifetime. Therefore, they will endeavor to exercise the central channel and Chi-Practice before doing the actual couple-practice of copulation. For example, the Dalai Lama claims:

> The experiences that you have while falling asleep and while dying result from the dissolution of the various elements. There are different ways in which this process of dissolution takes places. For instance, it can occur as a result of specific forms of meditation that employ the imagination. The dissolution, or withdraw, of the elements corresponds to levels of subtleties of consciousness. Whenever this dissolution occurs, there is one common element: the differences in the subtlety of consciousness occur due to changes in the vital energies.
>
> There are three ways that these changes in the vital energies can occur. One is a purely natural, physiological process, due to the dissolution of the different elements, namely earth (solidity), water (fluidity), fire (heat), and air (motility). It happens naturally in sleep and in the dying process, and it's not intentional. An analogous change occurs in the vital energies as a result of meditation that uses the power of concentration and imagination. This change in the vital energies results in a shift of consciousness from gross to subtle. The third way is through **sexual intercourse.** However, the shift of energies, and the shift from gross to subtle consciousness, does not occur in ordinary copulation, **but only through a special practice where one controls the movement of the regenerative fluid in sexual intercourse, both for men and women.** (Francisco J. Varela, *Sleeping, Dreaming and Dying*, Wisdom Publications, Boston, 1997, p.43-44.)

This statement from the Dalai Lama clearly shows: The lamas diligently exercise the central channel and Chi-Practice in order to practice the Highest Yoga Tantra through "the

功、中脈，就是要透過「性交行為」來修無上瑜伽，他們希望未來能夠透過練氣功、修中脈的方法，使得自己能在無上瑜伽雙身法中持久不洩；因此修氣功和盤腿跳躍都是為了修雙身法而準備的，以便在與女信徒坐姿合抱行淫時跳躍，使女信徒快速到達性高潮，才能輪座雜交而使所有女信徒都很快樂，達成「**博愛**」的目的；有這樣的性愛功夫，才能「愛盡天下女人」。在達賴喇嘛書中所說的「特定的修持」，其實就是「性愛修行法」，達賴喇嘛在書中有這麼說：

> ……我們討論的是光明的本初覺性，而且我們可以使用科學的方法來探知它的存在。
>
> 例如，從事一般性交行為的平凡男女，其生殖液的移動，**大大不同於從事性交行為的高度得證瑜伽士和瑜伽女**。儘管這男人和女人的生理構造不盡相同，但是從生殖液開始流下直到某個特定部位的時候，應該還是有相似的地方。平凡人的性交行為與高度得證密續修行人的性交行為，生殖液都會流到生殖器的部位，差別在於是否能控制生殖液的流動。**密續修行人被要求必須能控制生殖液的流動，所以經驗豐富的修行人甚至可以讓生殖液逆流，即使當它已經抵達生殖器的尖端時也不例外。**經驗較不豐富的修行人就得在離尖端較遠處便使它逆流，因為如果生殖液流到太近尖端的位置，會比較難控制。
>
> 有種方法可以訓練控制力，那是**將吸管插入生殖器，瑜伽士先透過吸管把水吸上去，然後吸牛奶，藉以增強性交時生殖液逆行的能力。**經驗豐富的修行人不僅可以從非常低的位置讓生殖液逆行，也可以**讓生殖液回到頭頂的部位，即生殖液原來降下來的地方。**（達賴喇嘛著，楊書婷、姚怡平

behavior of sexual intercourse." They hope that, through the methods of exercising the Chi-Practice and central channel, they can maintain longer duration without ejaculation during the Couple-Practice Tantra of the Highest Yoga Tantra. Thus, the Chi-Practice and jumping in a cross-legged sitting posture are prepared for the couple-practice of copulation. The *lamas* jump while embracing and copulating with the female follower and make her rapidly achieve orgasm. In this way, while having sex with multiple partners at the same time, the lamas can make all the female followers highly pleasurable and achieve the purpose of "**love for all.**" With such a technique of sexual love, they can "love all the females in the world." The "special practice" mentioned in the books of the Dalai Lama is actually "the practice method of sexual love." In a book by Francisco J. Varela, the Dalai Lama says as follows:

> Here we are discussing the effulgent pristine awareness, and it's quite feasible that its existence might be means of scientific research.
>
> For instance, there's a great difference between the movement of the regenerative fluids for two individuals engaged in ordinary sexual intercourse as opposed to **a highly realized male *yogi* and female *yogini* who are engaged in sexual intercourse.** Although there is a general difference, there should be similarities from the time when the regenerative fluids begin to flow down until they reach a certain point. In both ordinary sexual intercourse and **in the sexual union practiced by advanced Tantric practitioners,** the regenerative fluids move to the point of the genitals. Because of this it would be possible to conduct research to learn about the processes occurring in the ordinary sexual act.
>
> In principle, the general difference between the two types of sexual act is the control of the flow of regenerative fluids. **Tantric practitioners must have control over the flow of the fluids, and those who are highly experienced can even reverse the direction of the flow, even when it has reached the tip of the genitals.** Less experienced practitioners have to reverse the direction of the flow from a higher point. If the fluids descend too far down, they are more difficult to control.
>
> One training method that can be used as a standard of measurement of the level of one's control entails **inserting a straw into the genitals. In this practice the *yogi* first draws water, and later milk, up through the straw. That cultivates the ability to reverse the flow during intercourse.** Those who are highly experienced can not only reverse the flow from quite a low point, but

譯，《達賴：心與夢的解析》，2004 年 12 月出版，四方書城有限公司，頁 174-175。）

這裡提到，他們勤練氣功的方法就是「**將吸管插入生殖器，瑜伽士先透過吸管把水吸上去，然後吸牛奶，藉以增強性交時生殖液逆行的能力**。經驗豐富的修行人不僅可以從非常低的位置讓生殖液逆行，也可以**讓生殖液回到頭頂的部位，即生殖液原來降下來的地方**。」這其實就是採陰補陽，藉女人的身體來增強自己的身體。但是他們這個說法乃是自欺欺人，因為他們就算真的有這個功夫，能夠射出又吸回，也只是吸入膀胱內，稍後還是要與尿液一起排出體外；所以這是他們唬弄眾生的說法，並非如他們所說的吸回原來的處所或頭頂，一切有智慧的醫師都可以證明這個事實。其實現代所有喇嘛們都沒有吸回身中的能力，達賴自己也沒有這個能力，依他們自己的說法，都是不應該與女信徒合修雙身法的，達賴卻放縱這些全無實修雙身法資格的喇嘛們，繼續大量淫亂台灣女性。縱使他們將來有能力在射出精液以後，重新吸回身中，仍然是吸回膀胱中，不是達賴謊稱的吸回原來儲存精液的處所；最後還是要經由排尿而漏洩於體外，所以練成吸回功夫以後，還是一場空，最後依舊是白忙一場，根本不可能益壽延年。

再者，這些喇嘛們勤練氣功的目的，就是要把性能力加強，好讓他們能夠長久處於性交狀態中，免得太早射精。有時因為與女信徒修雙身法的過程太過猛烈，他們就得要練習盤腿跳躍，透過這樣跳躍的方式，來使女信徒快速進入性高潮中，也讓性交過程中產生樂觸的氣往兩腿散去，免得因為太興奮而提早射精；待氣散去之後，再繼續進行無上瑜伽的雙身性交。達賴喇嘛書中也這樣說：

The various systems of Highest Yoga Tantra seek to manifest the mind they can **draw the fluid back up to the crown of the head, from which it originally descended.** (Francisco J. Varela, *Sleeping, Dreaming and Dying*: Wisdom Publications, Boston, 1997, p.171-172.)

The above statements mention that their training method is to "**insert a straw into the genitals. In this practice the *yogi* first draws water, and later milk, up through the straw. That cultivates the ability to reverse the flow during intercourse.** Those who are highly experienced cannot only reverse the flow from quite a low point, but **they can draw the fluid back up to the crown of the head,** from which it originally descended." This is actually a way of taking the vital energy from the female to nourish the male, namely to strengthen one's body by means of the female body. However, their statements are actually deceiving themselves as well as others. Even if they do have the skill to draw the regenerative fluid back after ejaculation, it is only back into the bladder, and later, it will come out of the body with the urine. Therefore, their statements only show how they deceive people. It is not that, as they claim, the fluid is drawn back into the original place or the crown of the head. All the wise medical doctors can prove this fact. In fact, all the modern lamas, including the Dalai Lama, are incapable of drawing the regenerative fluid back into the bladder. According to their rule, they should not do the couple-practice of copulation with the female followers. However, the Dalai Lama indulges those lamas who are unqualified for the real couple-practice to continue to have sex with the Taiwanese females. Even if the lamas are capable of drawing the semen back into the body after ejaculation, it is back into the bladder, but not into the original place where the semen is stored, which is a lie from the Dalai Lama. Supposing the semen can be drawn back into the bladder, it will finally come out of the body with the urine. Therefore, even if they have the skill to draw the semen back, it still ends up with nothing and is impossible to prolong one's life.

Moreover, the purpose of the lamas' diligent practice of Chi is to increase their sexual ability so that they can maintain the sexual intercourse for a longer time, avoiding premature ejaculation. Sometimes, because the couple-practice of copulation with the female followers is too vigorous, they have to practice jumping in a cross-legged sitting posture; through such a way of jumping, they make the female followers achieve orgasm rapidly and also let the Chi of pleasurable sensation produced during the sexual intercourse fade out along the two thighs, avoiding premature ejaculation because of too much excitement; after the Chi fades out, they continue to do the couple-practice of copulation of the Highest Yoga Tantra. In a book of the Dalai Lama, it claims:

The various systems of Highest Yoga Tantra seek to manifest the mind of

of clear light, also called the fundamental innate mind of clear light, by way of different techniques. One of these techniques is **to use blissful orgasm (but without emission)** to withdraw the grosser levels of consciousness, thereby manifesting the most subtle level of mind.
（The XIV Dalai Lama, *Kalachakra Tantra: Rite of Initiation,* Wisdom Publications, Boston, 1989, p.35.）

　　中文語譯如下：【各種無上瑜伽密續的方法都是要經由各種不同的技巧去顯現明光心，也叫作本俱的基礎明光心，這些技巧其中之一就是**使用性高潮的大樂**（但是沒有射精）來去除較粗層次的意識，經由這樣的方法就可以顯現最微細層次的心。】

　　因此達賴喇嘛所弘揚的藏傳「佛教」，本質就是要與女信徒性交，但是他們希望能夠長時間性交，因此規定不能射精（除非為了替弟子做密灌頂時需要使用「甘露」，才會射精以後再從女弟子的女陰中收集淫液），因為射精以後就無法繼續修無上瑜伽的性交雙身法了，故達賴喇嘛又說：

> 依據密續的解釋，樂的經驗得自三種狀況：一是射精，二是**精液在脈中移動**，三是**永恆不變的樂**。密續修行利用後二種樂來證悟空性。因為利用樂來證悟空性的方法非常重要，所以我們發現無上瑜伽續觀想的佛都是與明妃交合。
> （達賴喇嘛文集（3）──《西藏佛教的修行道》頁 85。）

　　所以密宗信徒於「生起次第」都要努力的修氣功、盤腿跳躍，甚至如性變態的自虐狂一般，而將性器官插入吸管來練習吸引液體，目的就是要為未來與女信徒合修無上瑜伽性交雙身法而做準備。詳細內容，請看下一節的討論。然而探究密宗這樣的樂空雙運所獲得的全身大樂，卻與佛法中的阿羅漢道斷我見、斷我執完全無

clear light, also called the fundamental innate mind of clear light, by way of different techniques. One of these techniques is **to use blissful orgasm (but without emission)** to withdraw the grosser levels of consciousness, thereby manifesting the most subtle level of mind. (The XIV Dalai Lama, *Kalachakra Tantra: Rite of Initiation*, Wisdom Publications, Boston, 1999, p.35.)

Hence, the essence of Tibetan "Buddhism" propagated by the Dalai Lama is to have sex with the female followers. However, they hope that they can have sexual intercourse for a longer time, so ejaculation is not permitted. (Unless the "nectar' is required for the disciples to receive the secret empowerment, the lama will ejaculate and collect the obscene fluid from the vagina of the female disciple.) It is because, after ejaculation, one cannot continue the couple-practice of copulation of the Highest Yoga Tantra. Therefore, the Dalai Lama says again:

> According to the Tantric explanation, when we speak of a blissful experience here, we are referring to the bliss that is derived from the emission of the element of regenerative fluid, another type of bliss which is derived from **the movement of that element within the channels,** and a third type of bliss which is derived through **the state of immutable bliss.** In Tantric practice it is the two latter types of bliss that are utilized for realizing emptiness. Because of the great significance of utilizing bliss in the realization of emptiness we find that many of the meditational deities in Highest Yoga Tantra are in union with a consort.
>
> (HH the Dalai Lama, *A Survey of the Paths of Tibetan Buddhism,* PDF edition, p.27.
>
> retrieved from http://www.lamayeshe.com/index.php?sect=article&id=421, 2010/01/10)

Hence, in the "generation stage," the Tantric followers have to endeavor to do the Chi-Practice, practice jumping in a cross-legged sitting posture and even insert the straw into the genitals, like a masochist, to practice drawing back the fluid. The purpose of such practices is to prepare for the future couple-practice of copulation (the Highest Yoga Tantra) with the female followers. For detailed information, please refer to the discussions in the following chapter. However, the investigation into the whole-body bliss obtained from the Tantric Dual Operations of Bliss and Emptiness shows that it has nothing to do with the eliminations of self-view and self-attachment in the Buddhist practice of attaining Arhatship; it also has nothing to do with the emptiness-nature realized by bodhisattvas in Buddhism. It is because the emptiness-nature realized by bodhisattvas is the eighth *vijnana* Tathagatagarbha, while the emptiness mentioned by the Dalai Lama is only the conscious cognizing mind in the whole-body bliss. Only because the conscious cognizing

關；也與佛法中的菩薩所證空性完全無關，因爲菩薩所證的空性是第八識如來藏心，而達賴所說的空性只是全身大樂中的意識覺知心，只因爲受樂中的意識覺知心不是物質，就謊稱爲佛法中所說的空性。所以西藏密宗是以假代眞的假佛法，他們自古至今都沒有人證過空性。

而「藏傳佛教——喇嘛教」還另外規定每日努力修雙身法，而能達到無上瑜伽第四喜的性高潮階段全身遍樂而不射精；但是藏密的修行人，得要抱著女人保持這個性高潮樂觸，至少得要每天都保持長達八個時辰（也就是現代人說的十六個小時）之久，因此他們才要努力的修拙火、氣功、寶瓶氣……等法，讓自己不會早早射精而每天長時間抱著女人受樂。學密的女人則是要每天抱著男人交合，長時間處於性高潮中。這在藏密喇嘛教中格魯派（俗稱黃教）所謂的「至尊」宗喀巴所著《密宗道次第廣論》中有這樣說：

> ……若傳女子灌頂，於金剛處當知爲蓮。此如妙吉祥、〈口授論〉第三灌頂時云：「由虛空界金剛合，具正眼者生大樂，若於正喜離欲喜，見二中間遠離堅，蓮空金剛摩尼寶，蓮藏二合金剛趺，若時見心入摩尼，知彼安樂即爲智，此是圓滿次第道，最勝師長共宣說。貪離貪中皆無得，刹那妙智於彼顯，八時一日或一月，年劫千劫受此智。」正灌頂時受須臾頃，正修習時長時領受經八時等。（《密宗道次第廣論》宗喀巴著，法尊法師譯，妙吉祥出版社 1986/6/20 精裝版，頁 384。）

在宗喀巴的《菩提道次第廣論》後半部的止觀中，也是一樣的說法；只是用語很隱晦，讓外行人讀不懂。

達賴喇嘛的老祖宗宗喀巴在《密宗道次第廣論》中所說：「刹

mind in the bliss is not material, they lie that the conscious mind is the emptiness-nature in the Buddha dharma. Therefore, Tibetan Buddhism is a fake Buddhism that replaces the real with the false. The Tibetan Tantric practitioners have never realized the emptiness-nature from the ancient time till now.

In "Tibetan Buddhism," another rule is to diligently do the couple-practice of copulation every day and can attain the state of orgasm in the fourth joy of the Highest Yoga Tantra with the whole-body bliss, yet without ejaculation. The Tibetan Tantric practitioners have to embrace the female and maintain the pleasurable sensation of orgasm for at least eight double-hours (sixteen hours) a day; thus, they endeavor to practice the methods of inner heat (*kundalini*), the Chi-Practice, Vase-Chi, etc. so that they will not have early ejaculation while embracing the female with pleasurable sensation for a long time every day. The female Tantric practitioners have to embrace and copulate with the male, staying in the state of orgasm for a long time. In the *Extended Treatise on the Progression of the Esoteric Path* authored by Tsongkhapa, so-called the "Most Honorable" of the Gelug Sect (commonly called Yellow Hat Sect) in Tibetan Lamaism, it claims:

> ... If the empowerment is transmitted to a female, one should make her know the *vajra* place refers to the lotus. This is like the wondrous favor, as in the third empowerment of *The Orally Taught Treatise* says: "Because of the *vajra* union with the realm of infinite space, the bliss arises in one who has the correct eye. If one can be away from the joy of desire during the joy of orgasm, one sees the middle that is away from the two sides, and it becomes stiff. The lotus emptiness and the *vajra mani* are jewels; the lotus and the *mani* are joined together in *vajra* cross-legged sitting posture. When one sees the *citta* reaches the *mani,* one understands that the peaceful joy is the wisdom. This is the perfect way in stages, which is expounded by all the supreme teachers. In the states of greed and being away from greed, both are nothing obtainable. The instant wondrous wisdom become manifest on that condition. One receives the wisdom for **eight double-hours (sixteen hours) a day, a whole day, a month, a year, an eon or a thousand eons.**" While receiving the empowerment, one enjoys a short-term pleasure. While in actual practice, one enjoys the pleasure for eight double-hours a day, etc. (Tsongkhapa, *Extended Treatise on the Progression of the Esoteric Path,* translated into Chinese by dharma-master Fazun, Wondrous Favor Publishing Co., 1986, p.384.)

It says the same under the topic of Samatha and Vipassana (Tranquility and Insight) in the second half of his another book, *The Great Treatise on the Stages of the Path to Enlightenment (LamRim)*;

那妙智於彼顯，八時一日或一月，年劫千劫受此智」就是說，宗喀巴告訴他的弟子（即歷代達賴喇嘛等藏傳假佛教信徒）在無上瑜伽雙身法進行中，男女二根交合之剎那間生起第四喜的樂觸，這個叫作「妙智慧」；這個「妙智慧」在喇嘛上師與女信徒佛母彼此淫交苟合之際就會顯現出來，已受密宗自創的三昧耶戒的密宗男女行者，應當每日至少八個時辰（即十六個小時），或全天，都是在此男女性交的樂觸之中安住；甚至於要維持整整一個月或者整整一年、整整一劫，乃至整整一千劫之中，都要保持在男女性交的樂觸中安住。我們姑且不管古今藏傳假佛教—喇嘛教—的所有活佛喇嘛們是否能做到（實際上連宗喀巴自己都做不到，更不用說歷代早夭的達賴喇嘛），因爲這是宗喀巴的癡心妄想，連他自己都做不到，後代的活佛喇嘛就更別說了。按照宗喀巴的規定，所有修雙身法的喇嘛們，要不斷地在第四喜樂觸之交合快樂中，在正受性交樂空雙運的一念不生樂觸中，讓覺知心保持一念不生，此時的覺知心無形無色，即是空性，這已經是落入常見外道境界中，不是佛法中說的證空性；又說此爲妙智慧，與佛法中說的解脫道智慧及佛菩提智慧無關。這樣荒唐的主張，完全背離佛教的解脫眞理，也違背佛教戒律的規範。規定喇嘛們必須日日淫樂的三昧耶戒，乃是欲界最低下的淫樂境界，他們根本不能持守如來傳授的在家五戒、小乘比丘戒、比丘尼戒、大乘菩薩戒，而是陷害眾生一起造作下墮惡道的邪淫惡業，都是破壞家庭、破壞清淨佛戒的假佛教，頂多只是世間性愛藝術的學習者與推廣者。

however, obscure or ambiguous terms are used, and it is difficult for the laymen to understand.

In the *Extended Treatise on the Progression of the Esoteric Path,* Tsongkhapa claimed: "The instant wondrous wisdom becomes manifest on that condition. One receives the wisdom for eight double-hours (sixteen hours) a day, a whole day, a month, a year, an eon or a thousand eons." Namely, Tsongkhapa told his disciples (i.e. the followers of Tibetan fake Buddhism such as all the Dalai Lamas of successive generations) that, during the couple-practice of copulation (the Highest Yoga Tantra), the pleasurable sensation of the fourth joy arising instantly from the union of male and female sex organs is called "wondrous wisdom." This "wondrous wisdom" will become manifest when the lamas or gurus copulate with their female followers (or called buddha-mother). The Tantric male or female practitioners who have taken the *samaya* precepts, which were invented by Lamaism, should dwell securely in the pleasurable sensation of sexual intercourse at least eight double-hours (i.e. sixteen hours) a day or a whole day. Even more, they should keep dwelling in the pleasurable sensation of sexual intercourse for a whole month, a whole year, a whole eon or even a whole thousand eons. All ancient and present living-buddhas or lamas of Tibetan fake Buddhism are incapable of achieving such a state. (In fact, even Tsongkhapa himself was unable to do it, not to mention those Dalai Lamas of successive generations who died in their early age.) It is because this is a delusional thought of Tsongkhapa; he even could not do it himself, let alone the living-buddhas or lamas of later generations. According to the rule by Tsongkhapa, all the lamas who practice the couple-practice of copulation should continuously maintain the conscious mind in a state where no thought arises while they are in the fourth joy of pleasurable union or the Dual Operations of Bliss and Emptiness during the sexual intercourse. The perceptive mind at that time is shapeless and formless, and it is falsely claimed to be the emptiness-nature, which has fallen into the state of non-Buddhist eternalism and is not the emptiness-nature realized in Buddhism. The so-called wondrous wisdom by them has completely nothing to do with the Buddhist wisdom of the Liberation-Way and the Buddhahood-Way. Such a ridiculous claim completely deviates from the truth of Buddhist liberation and violates the Buddhist precepts. The *samaya* precept stipulates that the lamas should take the obscene pleasure, which is the lowest state in the desire-realm, every day. It is impossible for them to keep the precepts transmitted by Tathagata such as the lay five precepts, the Hinayana Bhiksu precepts and Bhikshuni precepts, as well as the Mahayana Bodhisattva precepts. On the contrary, they are making the sentient beings collectively create the evil karma of adultery that will lead to the evil paths. Tibetan Buddhism is a fake Buddhism that destroys family and violates the pure Buddhist precepts. At most, they are learners and promoters of the art of worldly sexual love.

上圖是藏傳假「佛教」—喇嘛教—的男女立姿性交冒充「成佛」的雙身像。

The above picture is the couple-practice of copulation in standing posture, a couple-body statue of Tibetan fake "Buddhism," or called Lamaism; they falsely claim to have attained Buddhahood.

乙、博愛
──就是與女信徒廣泛性交的無上瑜伽樂空雙運

　　藏傳假佛教無上瑜伽（樂空雙運）號稱是最究竟的佛法，但這只是喇嘛們一廂情願的說法，真正的佛法從來就不是這樣。而喇嘛教無上瑜伽（樂空雙運）的本質是什麼呢？說穿了就是要**博愛**，要「**與年輕貌美的女信徒廣泛而無保留地一一性交**」，使美貌年輕的所有女信徒，都與喇嘛們長時間共同住在性高潮中，這才是達賴喇嘛一直掛在嘴上的**博愛**的真正意思。有這種長時間保持性高潮的聰明智慧，也願意使所有女人都在與自己性交時，一一達到性高潮而且獲得長時間的快樂，才是達賴喇嘛所說的**慈悲**。達賴喇嘛在書中這麼說：

> 具有堅定**慈悲**及**智慧**的修行者，可以在修行之道上運用**性交**，以**性交**做為強大意識專注的方法，然後顯現出本有的澄明心。目的是要實證及延長心的更深刻層面，然後用此力量加強對空性的了悟。（達賴喇嘛著，《達賴生死書》，第一版第五次印行，天下雜誌股份有限公司，頁157。）

他又在其他書中說：

> 根據新譯派，修秘密真言到某種程度時，修者修特殊法，如利用**性伴侶**、打獵等等。雖然利用**性伴侶**之目的，不難被說成是為了用欲於道及引出較細的證空之識。（達賴喇嘛著，《慈悲與智見》，1997年3月修版三刷，羅桑嘉措──西藏兒童之家，頁246。）

　　很顯然，喇嘛們是利用女信徒作為性伴侶，進行廣泛性交的實踐，美其名為「加強對空性的了悟」，實際上就是要與大多數女信徒性交，假借佛法中「了悟」的名相來誘拐年輕貌美的女人與上師喇嘛性交（實際上卻拒絕與年長不美的女信徒性交，違背博愛的精神）。達賴喇嘛這個要利用性伴侶的假佛法，在他的英文本書中是這樣說的：

2 Love for All—Having sexual love with many female followers for the Dual Operations of Bliss and Emptiness of the Highest Yoga Tantra

The Tibetan fake Buddhism claims that the Highest Yoga Tantra (the Dual Operations of Bliss and Emptiness) is the most ultimate Buddha dharma. However, it is only the lamas' wishful thinking. The real Buddha dharma can never be like that. What is the essence of the Lamaistic Highest Yoga Tantra (the Dual Operations of Bliss and Emptiness)? To be frank, it is to **have love for all**, to **"have sexual love with all the beautiful young female followers one by one."** The true meaning of **love for all** from the Dalai Lama is to make all the beautiful young female followers and lamas dwell in the state of orgasm together. To have the smart wisdom of maintaining orgasm for a long duration and to be willing to make all the females achieve orgasm with happiness for a long time during sexual intercourse are actually the **compassion** told by the Dalai Lama. In his book, the Dalai Lama says:

> A practitioner who has firm **compassion** and **wisdom** can **make use of sexual intercourse** in the spiritual path as a technique for strongly focusing consciousness and manifesting the fundamental innate mind of clear light. Its purpose is to actualize and prolong the deeper levels of mind in order to put their power to use in strengthening the realization of emptiness. (Dalai Lama XIV/translated and edited by Jeffrey Hopkins, *Mind of Clear Light: Advice on living well and dying consciously,* Atria Books, 2003, p.176.)

He says again in his another book:

> According to the New translation Schools, at a certain high point in the practice of Secret Mantra, the mantrika engages in special practices such as making use of a **sexual partner**, hunting animals, and so forth. Though it is easy to explain the purpose of employing a partner as a means of bringing desire to the path and inducing subtler consciousnesses which realize emptiness, the hunting of animals cannot be explained that way. (The XIV Dalai Lama, *Kindness,*

According to the New translation Schools, at a certain high point in the practice of Secret Mantra, the mantrika engages in special practices such as making use of a **sexual partner**, hunting animals, and so forth. Though it is easy to explain the purpose of employing a partner as a means of bringing desire to the path and inducing subtler consciousnesses which realizing emptiness, the hunting of animals cannot be explained that way.

（The XIV Dalai Lama, *Kindness, Clarity, & Insight,* Snow Lion Publications, 1988, p. 219.）

我們按照英文本語譯如下：【**根據新譯派，秘密真言**(Secret Mantra)**修行的某一高點**(high point)**，真言行者**(mantrika)**從事一些特別的修行如利用性伴侶、打獵等等。雖然很容易解釋使用性伴侶是為了引發欲望到修行之路以及包括體悟空的微細意識，但打獵就不能這樣解釋。】**

因此很明確的知道，達賴喇嘛就是要利用性伴侶來達到無上瑜伽雙身法性交的目的，其實這就是達賴喇嘛所弘揚藏傳假佛教的最終目的。在達賴喇嘛另外一本書中也有同樣的說法：

由上所述，修根本心的方式就有三種：（1）依新派對《秘密集會》的解說；（2）依《時輪密續》的空相等說法；以及（3）依寧瑪的大圓滿法。根據新派的說法，在修習秘密真言達到某種高程度時，真言行者可以修特別的法門，如**利用性伴侶以及獵殺動物等**。雖然雇用性伴侶的目的，可以容易地解釋成是一種引貪欲入道的手段，並且也為了誘使證空的較細意識生起，不過，獵殺動物卻無法如此解釋。（達賴·喇嘛十四世著，黃啟霖譯，《圓滿之愛》，1991/09/01 初版一刷，時報文化出版企業有限公司，頁322。）

因此達賴的書中說明得很清楚，喇嘛教的秘密真言修行，最後得要找性伴侶來實修，其實就是要與女信徒性交，但是達賴喇嘛最後還故意說：「不過，獵殺動物卻無法如此解釋。」這是他們的障眼法，

Clarity, & Insight, Snow Lion Publications, 1988, p.219.)

Obviously, the lamas are using the female followers as the sexual partners to have the practice of extensive copulations. They give it a dignified name and say that it is to "strengthen the realization of emptiness." Actually, the gurus or lamas desire to have sex with most of the female followers; under the guise of Buddhist term "enlightenment," they seduce the beautiful young females. (In fact, they refuse to have sex with the ugly old females, violating the spirit of love for all.) What the Dalai Lama preaches is "a fake Buddhism that makes use of sexual partners."

Therefore, it is clearly understood that the Dalai Lama makes use of sexual partners to achieve the purpose of the couple-practice of copulation of the Highest Yoga Tantra, which is actually the final goal of Tibetan fake Buddhism preached by the Dalai Lama. Therefore, in the books of the Dalai Lama, it explains very clearly that the practice of the Secret Mantra in Lamaism needs to have an actual practice with a sexual partner eventually. It actually needs to have sex with the female followers, but the Dalai Lama purposely says in the end: "..., the hunting of animals cannot be explained that way." This is a cover-up. Actually, they only use "the statement of hunting animals" as a cover for their practice of the Highest Yoga Tantra (the Dual Operations of Bliss and Emptiness) with sexual partners. In his another English book, the Dalai Lama claims:

> The three lower *tantras* do involve using in the bliss that arises upon looking at, smiling at, and holding hands or embracing a meditated Knowledge Woman (consort);(The XIV Dalai Lama, *Deity Yoga: In Action and Performance Tantra*, Snow Lion Publications, New York, 1981, p.211.)

Therefore, the lower level *tantras* involve the meditation on "looking at, smiling at, holding hands or embracing" a sexual partner. However, the higher *tantra* is to have an actual practice of the Highest Yoga Tantra with a real female follower; namely, their final goal is to have an actual couple-practice of copulation (the Highest Yoga Tantra) with female partners, the Dual Operations of Bliss and Emptiness that make both of the couple achieve orgasm. Hence, the

其實只是用「打獵的說法」來掩飾他們要找性伴侶來修無上瑜伽樂空雙運罷了！達賴在他其他英文著作中說：

The three lower tantras do involve using in the path the bliss that arises upon looking at, smiling at, and holding hands or embracing a meditated Knowledge Woman (consort); （The XIV Dalai Lama, *Deity Yoga: In Action and Performance Tantra,* Snow Lion Publications, New York, 1981, p. 211）

中文語譯如下：【三個較低階的密續確實使用在冥想和智慧女（明妃）（編案：就是性伴侶）之間的注視、微笑、牽手或擁抱而升起的大樂。】

因此低階的密續乃是用冥想與性伴侶之間的「注視、微笑、牽手、擁抱」，但是高階段的就是要找女信徒真槍實彈實修無上瑜伽，也就是說，他們最後的目的就是要與女伴實修雙身法無上瑜伽，要使雙方都達到性高潮的樂空雙運。因此達賴一再的在書中說要「性伴侶」，我們再舉一例，達賴喇嘛說：

……根據新譯派，修秘密真言到某種程度時，修者修特殊法，如利用性伴侶、打獵等等。（第十四世達賴喇嘛講述，《迎向和平》，慧炬出版社出版，達賴喇嘛西藏基金會印贈〈免費結緣〉，2002/7初版第二刷，頁 93。）

因此「性伴侶」對藏傳假佛教的喇嘛們而言，是一個非常重要的角色，由此也就明白為什麼他們常常會有強行性侵的事件發生——當女信徒不願意與喇嘛合修雙身法，而喇嘛當時誤以為女信徒是半推半就，強行性侵以後就會爆發出性侵害的醜聞。更多的是女信徒被「即身成佛」的說法迷惑，誤以為雙身法的樂空雙運是真佛法，所以被喇嘛誘惑而常常暗中與喇嘛合修雙身法，成為這些女信徒與喇嘛之間的永久秘密，她們的丈夫終其一生都不會知道內情。因為「藏傳佛教——

Dalai Lama repeatedly mentions **"the sexual partner"** in his books.

Therefore, for the lamas of Tibetan fake Buddhism, "the sexual partner" plays a very important role. For this reason, it is understood why they are often accused of sexual assaults—when the female follower is unwilling to have the couple-practice with the lama, and the lama mistakenly thinks that she only pretends to be shy, a scandal breaks after the lama has sexually assaulted her. And yet, more female followers are misled by the claim of "attaining Buddhahood in this lifetime," wrongly thinking that the couple-practice of copulation (the Dual Operations of Bliss and Emptiness) is real Buddhism. Therefore, the female followers are seduced by the lamas and have the couple-practice of copulation with the lamas privately. It is a forever secret between the female followers and the lamas; their husbands will never know the truth throughout their whole life. It is because "Tibetan Buddhism (Lamaism)" focuses on the couple-practice of copulation, which is their core doctrine and theory.

From the evidence of so many examples, we should notice why the Dalai Lama says **"making use of a sexual partner"** in many of his books. From the books of another Tantric *guru,* Yogi C.M. Chen, a famous great practitioner of White Hat Sect, we can find a more definite answer. Through his explanation, the readers can understand why the lamas of Tibetan "Buddhism" (Lamaism) need to have the couple-practice of copulation with the female followers. In a Chinese book of Yogi C.M. Chen, he said explicitly:

> You cannot just use the method of visualization. **An actual physical female is needed**, which is exactly what happens in the third empowerment. Why do you have to use an actual physical female but not a visualized one? It is because the physical conditions of a visualized female are not good enough (Editor's note: the physical conditions refer to the ejaculated semen and the union of two sex organs.) in comparison to those of an **actual physical one** (Editor's note: female consort). With an actual physical female, on a sublimated basis, one can have an actual practice and therefore gain the real wisdom. For

喇嘛教」就是搞「雙身法性交」的，這是他們的核心法義與思想。我們再從達賴喇嘛另外一段文字中，還是說要「**利用性伴侶**」，請看達賴喇嘛說：

> 根本心的修行方式是根據：（一）新譯派所講的「密集金剛密續」；（二）時輪空相法等等；（三）寧瑪派的大圓滿法。根據新譯派，修秘密真言到某種程度時，修者修特殊法，如**利用性伴侶**、打獵等等。雖然利用性伴侶之目的，不難被說成是為了用欲於道及引出較細的證空之識，……只有在這種崇高境界中，才能以悲心將瞋怒用於修道。是故，新譯派的此一修法之基，與大圓滿法之基相同。（第十四世達賴喇嘛講述，《迎向和平》，慧炬出版社出版，達賴喇嘛西藏基金會印贈〈免費結緣〉，2002/7，初版第二刷，頁 93-94。）

從這麼多的舉證來看，我們應當注意，為什麼達賴喇嘛在多本書或許多文字中都說「**利用性伴侶**」呢？我們可以再從另外一位密宗上師，也就是密宗有名的白教大修行人陳健民上師於其書中的說法，就可以獲得更為明確的答案；看到他的說明，讀者就能夠瞭解藏傳「佛教」─喇嘛教─為什麼非得要與女信徒一起修雙身法。在陳健民上師的書中，非常露骨的說：

> 你不單只用觀想，而且用**實體的**，用真正的女人，那麼就是第三灌。為什麼要用真正的女人而不只是觀想一個呢？因為觀想的他的物質條件（編案：物質條件是指射出的精液與兩性器官的交合）就不夠了。用**實體的**（編案：真實女人──明妃），那物質條件就很夠，他就等於有這個資本了，有這個被昇華的資本，有這個本錢。有這個本錢，然後才能真正的修，才真正有智慧。譬如你觀想個女的，你甚至觀來觀去，你**雞巴都硬不起來**。你要有個真正的女人，它就硬起來，他就搞起來，

example, although you try to visualize a female, over and over, you **still cannot get your penis stiff.** Once you have a real female, your penis becomes stiff and active in having sex, and can perform the real function. (Editor's note: the function that can ejaculate the semen, which is used as the nectar in secret empowerment) (C.M. Chen, *Yogi Chen's Literary Work Collections,* Vol. 1, edited by Xu Jinting, Samantabhadra Audio Publishing Co., 1991, p.238.)

These words are extremely rude and explicit, like the dirty words in lower class people; however, the description is rather frank and straight. The Dalai Lama conveys the same meaning in his book and says:

In Guhyasamaja, in the section related to entering into union with a consort, it is said that if the consort is an action seal, a **live consort,** visualizing deities on her body becomes an actual body *mandala* practice. But if one is entering into union with a **visualized consort, it does not.** (Dalai Lama XIV, *The Union of Bliss and Emptiness,* Snow Lion Publications, New York, 1988, p.73-74.)

From the above evidence, it is known that the essence of the Highest Yoga Tantra (the Dual Operations of Bliss and Emptiness) of Tibetan "Buddhism" is only to **"have sex with the female followers."**

The Dalai Lama and lamas of "Tibetan Buddhism" teach the followers to have **love for all** while doing the couple-practice of copulation. The **love for all** means that multiple couples undergo sexual intercourse at the same time; during the process, they change partners continuously and take turns having sexual intercourse with multiple partners; sometimes, there are nine females and nine lamas having sexual intercourse in turn like animal. In Tibetan Buddhism, it is called *vajra* partner-changing dharma assembly. During the process, they make all the participant females achieve orgasm with happiness. In this way, the couple-practice of copulation with multiple partners is propagated. All the qualified Lamaistic gurus should practice the Tantric empowerment of couple-practice of copulation. However, after such an actual practice, they will surely become the hell beings because of breaking the precepts. Therefore, the

它就發生真正的作用（編案：能射出精液作爲密灌甘露之作用）。
（陳健民著，徐芹庭編《曲肱齋全集》（一），普賢錄音有聲出版社，
1991/07/10 出版精裝本，頁 238。）

這是極盡粗魯與露骨的話，與市井俗人罵髒話一般，但卻很坦
白。達賴喇嘛也於其書中說同樣的意思，達賴說：

秘密集會檀陀羅裡，有關與明妃和合的章節中，說若與**實體
明妃**行樂空雙運，才會成就真正的身曼荼羅修行，如果僅與
觀想中的明妃行樂空雙運，則其**成就不大**。（達賴喇嘛著，《喜
樂與空無》，唵阿吽出版社，1998 年一版一刷，頁 137-138。）

由這些證據可知，藏傳「佛教」—喇嘛教—的無上瑜伽（樂空雙
運）的本質就只是要「**與女信徒性交**」罷了！

以達賴爲首的「藏傳佛教」喇嘛們，他們教導信眾修學雙身法時
講究**博愛**，乃是要進行多對男女配對同時交媾；在過程中要不斷交換
對象，一一輪流交媾雜交；有的時候多到九位女性與九位喇嘛，如同
畜生雜交一般，密宗稱之爲金剛輪座法會，這時要使所有參加的女人
都達到性高潮而獲得快樂。如此弘揚男女雜交的雙身法，凡受證爲喇
嘛教的上師，都應當修習密宗這樣的雙身法灌頂；但喇嘛們這樣實修
以後，都必然會成爲破戒的地獄人，所以達賴喇嘛的祈福不會有福可
得。而達賴喇嘛的祖師，號稱「至尊」的宗喀巴於《密宗道次第廣論》
卷十三說：

先供物請白者，以幔帳等隔成屏處，弟子勝解師爲金剛薩
埵，以具足三昧耶之智慧母，生處無壞，**年滿十二等之童女，
奉獻師長**。如〈大印空點〉第二云：「賢首纖長目，容貌妙
莊嚴，**十二或十六，難得可二十**，廿上爲餘印，令悉地遠

Dalai Lama's prayer will not bring the blessings to Taiwanese people. The "Most Honorable" Tsongkhapa, a patriarch of the Gelug lineage (to which the Dalai Lama belongs), said in the *Extended Treatise on the Progression of the Esoteric Path,* Vol. 13:

> Someone who ask the teacher for empowerment should make offerings first. A curtain is used as a screen. The disciple understands very well that the teacher is *vajrasattva.* Wisdom mothers with complete *samaya,* whose genitals are healthy and who are **virgins over the age of 12 etc., are offered to the teacher.** Just like the statement in the second chapter of *Sutra on Great-Seals:* "One should choose females who are most wise, virtuous, with slender eyes, having a wondrous dignified face, and **aged from 12 to 16, or 20 if difficult to obtain. Females over 20 are used in other seals** (*mudra*) because it will make all the stages of practice impossible to attain. One's sisters, daughters, or wife are offered to the teacher." (Tsongkhapa, *Extended Treatise on the Progression of the Esoteric Path,* translated into Chinese by dharma-master Fazun, Wondrous Favor Publishing Co., 1986, p.376)

Tsongkhapa thought the lamas should cooperate with the females to do the couple-practice of copulation (the Highest Yoga Tantra); after sexual intercourse, the lamas obtain the red and white *bodhicitta* (in fact, it is the mixture of obscene fluid from both sexes), which is used in the secret empowerment. Therefore, Tsongkhapa said:

> The last secret empowerment, which is transmitted to enable the disciple to expound the sutras, means the teacher and the nine female consorts attain the state all together. (Editor's note: namely, the lama teacher, so-called living-buddha, needs to copulate one by one with nine sexual partners, called female consorts, aged from 12 to 20; they achieve the orgasm of the fourth joy all together and observe the Union of Bliss and Emptiness; then, the lama teacher ejaculates the semen into the vagina of each female consort one by one and collect all the fluid mixture.) The *vajra*

離，姊妹或自女，或妻奉師長。」（《密宗道次第廣論》宗喀巴著，法尊法師譯，妙吉祥出版社 1986/06/20 精裝版，頁 376。）

宗喀巴認為，喇嘛應該與女人合作共修雙身法無上瑜伽，這樣性交完成後，就取得紅白菩提心（其實就是男女淫液的混和物），以之作為秘密灌頂之用，因此宗喀巴說：

為講經等所傳後密灌頂，謂由師長與自十二至二十歲九明等至（編案：也就是必須由師長喇嘛活佛與自十二歲至二十歲各種不同年齡之九位性伴侶明妃，一一與之交合而同入第四喜的性高潮中而觀樂空不二，而後一一射精於明妃下體中而收集之），俱種（編案：這樣具備九明之紅白菩提—上師與明妃混合後之淫液—俱有男女雙方之種子）金剛（編案：密宗說此淫液為金剛菩提心，是盜用佛法名相）注弟子口，依彼灌頂。如是第三灌頂前者，與一明（編案：與其中一明妃）合受妙歡喜。後者，隨與九明等至（編案：後者則是隨即與九位明妃同入性高潮中，這樣叫做九明等至），即由彼彼所生妙喜（編案：即由喇嘛與九位明妃一一行淫射精而取得與九位明妃混合的淫液，集合起來名為甘露而為弟子灌頂）。……（《密宗道次第廣論》宗喀巴著，法尊法師譯，妙吉祥出版社 1986/06/20 精裝版，頁 399-400。）

喇嘛們處處隱藏要「與女信徒性交」的目的，想要暗中繼續與所有美麗而年輕的女信徒性交；但是現代資訊發達，也有許多喇嘛於開示及著作中公開這個事實。例如 1938 年冬天，有一名西藏喇嘛教（即藏傳「佛教」）的一個名為更敦群培（Gedün Chöpel, 1905-1951）的喇嘛，寫了一本書名為《西藏慾經》，書中以大量的篇幅來介紹男女的性愛。（陳琴富中譯，台北：大辣出版社，2003，中文版譯自 Jeffrey Hopkins 的英譯本 Tibetan Arts of Love），英譯者 Jeffrey Hopkins 的說法，認為《西藏慾經》主要取材自著名的印度經典《愛經》（Kama Sutra）。根據《西藏慾經》

(Editor's note: Tibetan Buddhism claims that this obscene fluid is *vajra bodhicitta;* they misuse the Buddhist term.) possessing the seeds (Editor's note: the red and white *bodhi*, which is the obscene fluid mixture from the guru and nine female consorts, has the seeds of both sexes.) is put into the mouth of his disciple; in this way, the empowerment is performed. It is the third empowerment, or the former stage, in which the teacher and a female consort receive the wondrous joy together; then, in the latter stage, the teacher attains the state together with the **nine female consorts.** (Editor's note: in the latter stage, the teacher attains the state of sexual orgasm together with the nine female consorts, which is called attaining the state together with the nine female consorts.) The wondrous joys arise from them together. (Editor's note: namely, the lama has sex with the nine female consorts one by one and ejaculates the semen; together with the obscene fluid obtained collectively from the nine female consorts, the fluid mixture is called the nectar, which is used for the empowerment to the disciple.)... (Tsongkhapa, *Extended Treatise on the Progression of the Esoteric Path,* translated into Chinese by dharma-master Fazun, Wondrous Favor Publishing Co., 1986, p.399-400.)

The lamas try to hide the purpose of "**having sex with the female followers**" in all respects; they desire to keep on having sex with the beautiful young female followers in private. However, information spread widely in modern times. Many lamas have made this fact public in their teachings or books. For example, Gedün Chöpel (1905-1951), a lama of Tibetan Lamaism (Tibetan "Buddhism") finished a book *Treatise on Passion* in the winter of 1938. The English version of Gedün Chöpel's *Treatise on Passion* is *Tibetan Arts of Love.* The book talks extensively about sex love. Jeffrey Hopkins, the editor of *Tibetan Arts of Love*, thinks that Gedün Chöpel's *Treatise on Passion* comes mainly from the world-famous *Kama Sutra* of India. According to a brief book description, *Tibetan Arts of Love* "presents in lucid detail the sixty-four arts of love, divided into eight varieties of sexual play—embracing, kissing, pinching and scratching, biting, moving to and fro and pressing, erotic noises, role reversal, and positions of love-making. ... An over-arching focus is sexual ecstasy as a door to spiritual experience. ..."

內容簡介：

> 他的書清晰的呈現了六十四種情慾藝術的細節，分成八類的
> 性愛遊戲──擁抱、親吻、捏與抓、咬、來回移動與抽送、
> 春情之聲、角色轉換、交歡的姿勢。其形而上的焦點是：**性
> 喜樂是通往根本自性的一道心靈經驗之門。**

（資料來源：http://www.nownews.com/2003/03/14/1128-1424898.htm，

引用時間：2009/11/7）

　　由此更敦群培喇嘛出書教導性愛，已經把藏傳「佛教」是古代印度性力派的底細全部曝光；大家就可以知道達賴為首的藏傳「佛教」喇嘛們，每天掛在嘴上喊得震天價響的「博愛」，乃是「與所有年輕貌美的女信徒常常進行雙身法性交的無上瑜伽樂空雙運」，與佛法中說的斷我見、斷我執、斷淫慾而證羅漢果無關，也與諸佛菩薩傳授的明心與見性的智慧無關，根本不是佛法。

喇嘛們常常發生性醜聞的原因，是「藏傳佛教」的教義本質乃以性交為修行的宗教，美其名為男女雙修無上瑜伽。

(Retrieved from http://www.snowlionpub.com/html/product_711.html, 2009/11/7)

From Lama Gedün Chöpel's book that teaches sex love, it has revealed that Tibetan "Buddhism" originates from the Tantrism of ancient India. Therefore, it is known that the term "love for all" frequently mentioned by the Dalai Lama and lamas of Tibetan "Buddhism" means to "frequently have the couple-practice of copulation (the Highest Yoga Tantra, the Dual Operations of Bliss and Emptiness) with all beautiful young female followers." It has nothing to do with the realization of *arhat* in which one's self-view, self-attachment, and lustful desire are eliminated. It also has nothing to do with the wisdom of realizing of one's true mind and seeing the Buddha-nature. It is not the Buddha dharma at all.

The reason why the lamas have been frequently involved in sex scandals is that the doctrinal essence of "Tibetan Buddhism" is about using copulation as its practice method, in the dignified name of Couple-Practice Tantra of the Highest Yoga Tantra.

丙、冰山一角
——近年各地密宗喇嘛性醜聞的媒體報導一覽

1994 年 11 月 〈舊金山 Free Press〉報導《西藏生死書》作者索甲仁波切遭控告性侵害。一名婦女在美國加州山塔庫魯斯郡向法院提出一樁求償千萬美元的官司。她聲稱遭受到《西藏生死書》作者索甲仁波切的脅迫與性侵害。

2000 年 6 月 來自尼泊爾的拉秋仁波切，被控對一名婦人性侵害。

2001 年 6 月 尼泊爾籍楚姓喇嘛被張姓女子控告騙婚及詐欺。

2002 年 10 月 〈新明日報〉報導：（香港訊）女商人自爆與來自中國成都密宗大師義雲高發生性關係，聲稱還拍下交歡錄影帶。

2002 年 10 月 瑜伽老師向警方指控，遭由印度來台弘法的喇嘛圖登且曲性侵害。

2004 年 12 月 台灣籍喇嘛楊鎬，涉嫌連續對兩名女子性侵害。

2006 年 4 月 時尚摩登西藏活佛盛噶仁波切，遭北台科大教授江燦騰抨擊他在台亂搞男女關係。

2006 年 7 月 中國林喇仁波切在台弘法，藉機性侵多名女信徒。還說他的精液（甘露）吞下後可得到最高加持。

2007 年 4 月 自稱是達賴認證的活佛、來自西藏在台灣傳法的敦都仁波切以「雙修」為名，不只對女信徒性侵未遂，甚至還亂搞男女關係，有多名女子受害。

3 Tip of the Iceberg—An overall news review of sex scandals about Tantric lamas at different places in recent years

Nov. 1994, the Free Press SAN FRANCISCO reports: Sogyal Rinpoche, author of the *Tibetan Book of Living and Dying,* is accused of sexual abuse in a $10 million civil suit filed in Santa Cruz County Superior Court by a woman, who says Sogyal Rinpoche, author of the *Tibetan Book of Living and Dying*, "coerced" her into an intimate relationship.

Jun. 2000, Laqiu Rinpoche from Nepal was accused of sexual assault on a woman.

Jun. 2001, a lama surnamed Chu from Nepal was accused of marriage fraud and deceit by a woman surnamed Zhang.

Oct. 2002, Shin Min Daily News, news report from Hong Kong: A businesswoman said that she had sexual relationship with a Tantric guru Yi Yungao, who is from Chengdu, China. She also claimed that she had taken a video tape of their sexual activity.

Oct. 2002, a female yoga teacher told the police that she was sexually assaulted by Lama Tudeng Danqu, who came from India to Taiwan to preach the dharma.

Dec. 2004, Lama Yang Hao, a Taiwanese, was suspected of consecutive sexual assaults on two females.

Apr. 2006, Singa Rinpoche, a modern-fashioned Tibetan living-buddha, was criticized by Chiang Tsan-Teng, associate professor of Technology and Science Institute of Northern Taiwan: Singa Rinpoche sleeps around in Taiwan.

Jul. 2006, Linla Rinpoche, from mainland China, preached the dharma in Taiwan. He sexually assaulted many female followers by taking advantage of the situations and claimed that, if one swallowed his semen (the nectar), one can have the utmost blessings.

Apr. 2007, Dundu Rinpoche, who is from Tibet and claims to be a living-buddha certified by the Dalai Lama, propagated the dharma in Taiwan. Under the guise of "couple-practice," he not only tried to sexually abuse female followers, but also slept around; there were many female victims.

　　2008 年 3 月　出生印度的貝瑪堪仁波切與黃姓婦人於道場發生性關係遭婦人丈夫當場舉發。

　　以上資料是參考網路、〈自由時報〉及其他新聞媒體所刊載資料，2008年3月12日彙整列舉。

　　這些報導只是喇嘛性侵事件的冰山一角；被性侵的婦女極多，多數因爲遭到脅迫，或因恐懼遭致社會人士的異樣眼光而不敢公開舉發，所以唯有見到冰山的一角；然藏傳「佛教」—喇嘛教—的邪淫性侵本質是不爭的事實，因爲密宗的教義中規定：喇嘛們要在每一世中的每一天都與女人交合，來得到全身遍樂的境界。透過本書的分析舉證，就會知道：年輕有姿色的女人學密而期待喇嘛不會強行性侵或誘姦她，是一廂情願、癡心妄想。

貝瑪千貝喇嘛與女信徒被捉姦在床，原始畫面擷取自 TVBS 新聞台及蘋果日報。

Mar. 2008, Khenpo Pema Chopel Rinpoche, born in India, had sex with a married woman surnamed Huang in the practice center. Her husband caught their affair on the spot and reported it to the police.

The above data are listed with reference to Internet, Liberty Times and other news media on March 12, 2008.

These reports are only the tip of the iceberg about the lamas' sexual assaults. There are a lot of female sexual assault victims and many of them dare not make a public accusation because they are threatened or afraid of other people's prejudice. Therefore, only the tip of the iceberg is seen. However, it is an indisputable fact that the essence of Tibetan "Buddhism" (Lamaism) is adultery and sexual abuse because the Tantric doctrine has the rule that lamas should have copulation with the females every day in each lifetime to attain the state of the whole-body bliss. Through the analysis and examples in this book, we can understand: it is a pious wish that the lamas would not sexually abuse or seduce a beautiful yong female follower.

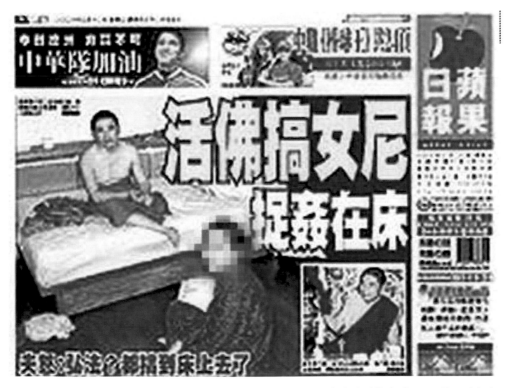

Khenpo Pema Chopel Rinpoche and a female follower were caught on the bed while having sex. The original pictures are retrieved from TVBS News and Apple Daily.

2006年7月15日／星期六　　自由時報　　社會焦點 B2

惡喇嘛詐財上億 性侵逾10人

女尼指控遭襲胸

多名女信眾跟尼姑昨日在台北市議員陪同下舉行記者會，控訴來自中國名為「林喇仁波切」的喇嘛，八年來不僅性侵多名女性，同時更假借募款名義詐財。

2006.07.15 新聞圖片（記者趙世勳攝）

林喇仁波切是來自中國四川省甘孜藏族自治州德格縣佐欽寺的住持

2007年7月24日／星期二

自由時報

B3 社會話題

性侵女尼 林喇仁波切被訴

女尼指據犯特徵 都吻合

藏傳「佛教」林喇仁波切，於 2007 年 7 月 24 日自由時報 B3 版面，報導其性侵新聞，而此喇嘛快速逃離台灣。密宗最初宣稱他是假喇嘛，後來被證明是大陸密宗某聞名寺院的住持以後，改口稱為「**偶發**事件」。

July 24, 2007, on the page B3, Liberty Times reports that Linla Rinpoche of Tibetan "Buddhism" committed sexual assaults, and he quickly left Taiwan. At first, the Tantric authorities claimed that he was a fake lama. Later, after he had been proved to be the abbot of a famous Tantric monastery, they changed their statement by saying that it was "an isolated incident."

四、達賴來台祈福各界報導

報導一

全球媒體關注達賴訪台　半島電視：帶來反效果

中評社台北 9 月 2 日電／今日新聞報導，達賴喇嘛 1 日在高雄舉行祈福法會，引發國際媒體高度關注，包括美國有線電視新聞網(CNN)，以及半島電視台等主要媒體，都加以報導。CNN報導有上萬人參加法會，而半島電視台則是在網站上指出，台灣邀請達賴來訪將使兩岸關係出現變化。

「我們首先報導台灣新聞，上萬人參加達賴所主持的莫拉克颱風罹難者祈福法會……」達賴 1 日在台灣的祈福法會，成為國際媒體報導的焦點，美國有線電視新聞網(CNN)也在整點新聞中加強報導，並指出中國大陸為了抗議達賴訪台，已取消部分官方訪台行程。

另外，新加坡電視台也報導達賴訪台，並邀請東亞事務專家丹尼李進行評論。丹尼李表示，達賴訪問並不會對兩岸關係造成太大的影響，「就長遠來看，我不認為達賴訪台會對兩岸關係造成影響，我想台灣和部分國際媒體在這方面都低估了北京對兩岸關係的重視。」

而半島電視台也在網路上報導達賴訪台，並表示這次的訪問將對台灣造成反效果，大陸方面甚至已經因此取消官員訪台活動。

（以上資料 2009/10/30 摘錄自：中國評論新聞網。
網址：http://www.chinareviewnews.com/crn-webapp/doc/docDetailCNML.jsp?
coluid=7&kindid=0&docid=101065229　引用時間：2009/11/08）

IV News Reports about the Dalai Lama's Taiwan Visit for Prayer

Report 1

Dalai Lama's Taiwan visit captures worldwide media attention. Al Jazeera: It will have a reverse effect.

September 2, Taipei, China Review News Agency, news reports today: The Dalai Lama held a prayer ceremony in Kaohisung on September 1. It draws the high attention of international media, including the major media such as CNN and Al Jazeera. CNN reports that over ten thousands people attended the prayer ceremony, while Al Jazeera says in the news network that the Dalai Lama's Taiwan visit will change the cross-strait relations.

"We first report the news from Taiwan: Over ten thousands people attended the prayer ceremony held by the Dalai Lama for the victims of Typhoon Morakot..." The Dalai Lama held a prayer ceremony in Taiwan on September 1, which has become the focus of international media. CNN has also especially reported in the Hourly News that the mainland China cancelled some of the officials' trips to Taiwan in protest at Dalai Lama's Taiwan visit.

In addition, Singapore TV also reported the Dalai Lama's visit to Taiwan and invited a specialist in the East-Asia affairs Denny Li for comments. Denny Li expressed his views that the Dalai Lama's visit will not have too much influence on cross-strait relations and he said, "On a long-term basis, I do not think the Dalai Lama's visit will have any influence on cross-strait relations. I think Taiwan and some of international media all underestimated the serious concern of Beijing about cross-strait relations."

Al Jazeera also reported the Dalai Lama's visit to Taiwan in the news network and said the Dalai Lama's visit will have a reverse effect on Taiwan, and mainland China has even cancelled the officials' trip to Taiwan because of this event.

(The above information is retrieved from China Review News, 2009/10/30
http://www.chinareviewnews.com/crn-webapp/doc/
docDetailCNML.jsp?coluid=7&kindid=0&docid=101065229
2009/11/08)

報導二

台佛教研究團體：達賴不是一位和平使者

中評社臺北 9 月 1 日電／西藏流亡精神領袖達賴喇嘛來台第三天，1 日上午在高雄巨蛋舉行祈福法會，下午則是演講，但兩場活動都有民眾在場外嗆聲抗議。上午，臺灣佛教研究團體臺灣正覺教育基金會有逾百位成員聚集在巨蛋門口，高舉黃色布條，抨擊密宗喇嘛蹂躪婦女、騙財騙色，達賴喇嘛不是一位和平使者。

正覺教育基金會董事楊順旭表示，修雙身法的喇嘛只是喇嘛教，達賴聲稱是藏傳佛教，但並非佛教。楊順旭認為，邪教比天災還可怕，很多人不明正邪，把專修雙身法、淫人妻女的喇嘛視為佛教的一支，還有人為其宣傳，誤導百姓跟著受累。

今日新聞報道，他表示，如果達賴真的關心臺灣災民，應該在印度幫忙募款，既然達賴沒有幫災民募款，他要求法會所獲得的收入，應該要捐給災民，而不是帶回印度，這才是真正為臺灣祈福。

（以上資料 2009/10/30 摘錄自：中國評論新聞網。
網址：http://cn.chinareviewnews.com/crn-webapp/doc/
docDetailCNML.jsp?coluid=7&kindid=0&docid=101064746
引用時間：2009/11/08）

報導三

場外抗議

達賴到台三天以來相繼受到不同名義的抗議，繼抵台首日受一反獨促統團體激烈抗議，以及昨日十餘名自稱災民者在酒店外抗議後，週二再度受到一群人士以宗教名義的抗議。

Report 2

Taiwanese Buddhist Research Groups: The Dalai Lama is not a messenger of peace

September 1, Taipei, China Review News Agency: On the third day in Taiwan, the Dalai Lama, the Tibetan exiled spiritual leader, held a prayer ceremony in the Kaohsiung Arena in the morning and gave a lecture in the afternoon. Both activities were met with howls of protest by the demonstrators outside the Arena. In the morning, over a hundred members of the True Enlightenment Education Foundation, a Taiwanese Buddhist Research Group, gathered in front of the gate of the Kaohsiung Arena. They displayed the yellow banners and criticized that the Tantric lamas sexually abuse the females, collect money by fraud, and are love swindlers; the Dalai Lama is not a messenger of peace.

Yang Shunxu, a director of the True Enlightenment Education Foundation, said that the lamas who do the couple-practice of copulation only belong to Lamaism, which the Dalai Lama claims to be Tibetan Buddhism. However, Lamaism is not Buddhism at all. Yang Shunxu thinks that the evil religion is more terrible than a natural disaster; many people are ignorant of right and evil; they wrongly consider Lamaism (its lamas focusing on the couple-practice of copulation and committing adultery with other people's wives or daughters) to be a branch school of Buddhism; some people still advertise Lamaism, misleading people and getting them into troubles.

In the news report today, Yang said, "If the Dalai Lama really cares about the victims of the disaster in Taiwan, he should help raise money in India. Since the Dalai Lama did not help raise money for the victims of the disaster, I request that the money raised from the prayer meeting should be given to the victims of the disaster but not brought back to India. This will be the true prayer for Taiwan."

(The above news information is retrieved from China Review News, 2009/10/30.
http://cn.chinareviewnews.com/crn-webapp/doc/
docDetailCNML.jsp?coluid=7&kindid=0&docid=101064746
2009/11/08)

Report 3

Protests Outside

The Dalai Lama has met with protests in different names since his arrival in Taiwan three days ago. After a strong protest from an anti-independence and

　　這群抗議人士在達賴上午於高雄巨蛋對災民祈福時，在場外四周高舉標語稱達賴屬喇嘛教並非佛教徒，組織抗議活動的孫正德對BBC中文網說，抗議者有三百人。

　　他們在場外對參加祈福法會的群眾發送反達賴宣傳單，有參加法會群眾指責他們是中共或國民黨派來，孫正德則否認其抗議是受政黨指使。

　　在台灣訪問的中國宗教局長葉小文此前針對達賴到訪說，不一定遠來的和尚才會念經，時事評論員林保華指出，這樣的說法是意圖挑動群眾鬥群眾。

　　孫正德說雖然其所屬的佛教團體在川震期間曾向中國宗教事務局捐款，但他們未直接與葉小文接觸，她並稱其抗議活動不是呼應葉小文。

（以上摘自BBC中文網 2009/09/01，駐台灣特約記者發自高雄）
（資料來源：多維新聞網
　網址：
　http://www.dwnews.com/big5/MainNews/Forums/BackStage/
　2009_9_1_12_44_33_365.html）

pro-reunification group on the first day of his arrival and a protest from more than ten alleged victims of the disaster outside the hotel yesterday, the Dalai Lama met with the protest again from a group of people in the name of religion on Tuesday.

While the Dalai Lama was holding a prayer ceremony for the victims of typhoon disaster in the Kaohsiung Arena this morning, these protesters displayed the banners saying that the Dalai Lama belongs to Lamaism but not Buddhism. Sun Zhengde, who staged this protest, said to BBC Chinese.com that there were three hundred protesters.

They handed out the anti-Dalai leaflets to the audience of the prayer meeting outside the Arena. Some participants in the prayer meeting criticized that they were incited by communist China or Kuomintang (KMT). Sun Zhengde negated that their protest was incited by any political party.

In response to the Dalai Lama's visit, Ye Xiaowen, head of the State Administration for Religious Affairs, China, currently visiting Taiwan, said that a foreign monk would not necessarily do a better job of praying. Lin Baohua, a commentator, pointed out that such a statement from Ye was to provoke people into a fight.

Sun Zhengde said, although her Buddhist community made a donation to the State Administration for Religious Affairs shortly after the Sichuan earthquake, they did not have any contact with Ye Xiaowen. She also claimed that their protest was not staged in response to Ye Xiaowen's statement.

(The above information is retrieved from BBC Chinese.com 2009/09/01,
 news report from Kaohsiung by a stringer in Taiwan.)

(Information source: DuoWei News
 http://www.dwnews.com/big5/MainNews/Forums/BackStage/2009_9_1_12_44_33_365.html)

附錄一、社會教育紀實：

出征略記
──記九月一日遠征高雄巨蛋向達賴喇嘛示威

─常喜此身非我有，隨緣應物行菩提─

從台北講堂出發

　　推廣組長宣布菩薩們遊覽車座次表，聲音低沉，一個個名字隨即融入講堂大樓前之暗夜中；台北百位身著白色唐裝的菩薩群，於漆黑天幕下醒目而沉寂。

　　巨型車輪迅疾滾動，平穩紮實地馳上征途。車上電子鐘顯示04:25，比預計遲了 25 分鐘。在車上即刻分發注意事項及重要聯絡電話。不久，隨著節奏的顛簸很快將大眾搖入夢鄉。望著窗外仍然靜謐的城市，腦中試著重組自己如何參與這件征戰的始末，不免疑惑未定行程之前已無法正常入眠，莫非往昔種子現行，連最後向主管請假都如順水推舟，而能成就此次南征之行。

　　車行順利，沿途自高雄持續有前勘部隊傳達訊息；到泰安休息站，天色轉亮，首度瞄見一位喇嘛鑽入賓士休旅車。征車再上路，推廣組長轉致講堂再三叮嚀之安全宣導注意事項，我們代表正覺菩薩眾，要時時注意身口意行；此次出動沒有個人，完全依止總指揮行誼。這是跨出正覺講堂，昭告天下，揭示正邪，石破天驚之舉。由於達賴行程屢屢變異，今日僅有巨蛋一場集會，下午即可返回講堂，講堂業已安排擇時播放ＤＶＤ講經，提供來不及趕回聽經的菩

Appendix A True Record of Social Education:

Initial Crusade

— A note of the demonstration against the Dalai Lama at the Kaohsiung Arena on September 1, 2009

—I rejoice in knowing that this physical body is not mine,
and practice the bodhi way, going with the flow of karmic conditions —

Departing from Taipei Lecture Hall (Northern Taiwan)

With a subdued soft voice, the Promotion Chief read out every participant's bus and seat numbers; her voice soon dissolved into the velvet darkness, which embraced the office building next to where we stood. We were a large group of one hundred participants — namely one hundred bodhisattvas, all dressed in white kung fu outfits, rather eye-catching in stark contrast to the black surroundings and the three big buses. We all remained stone silent.

The huge wheels whirled effortlessly and surely onto the highway, heading towards our destination. The digital clock read 04:25 a.m., twenty-five minutes behind our planned schedule. There was no minute to be wasted; an announcement regarding the crucial points of this trip was made right after the departure. Thereafter, sooner than anybody would notice, the rhythmical vast cradle rocked everybody into sleep; indeed, the previous night's short sleep was interrupted a few hours earlier. Leaning back against my seat and casting out into the completely quiet and dark city, I tried to recollect the whole picture of getting involved in this crusade. Somehow I did wonder, even before the agenda was finalized, I had not been able to sleep normally for a few nights already. Was it an omen that experiences from my past lives, "seeds of the deeds" as we call them, were being brought forth? Even my last minute leave request at work was accepted incredibly smoothly; it seemed like every detail worked in favor of my southward crusade.

We kept in close contact with the frontier team located in Kaohsiung City, as our journey progressed toward southern Taiwan. The morning sunlight broke out as we enjoyed our first break at Tai-An Refreshing Park. From the corner of my eyes, I spotted my first *lama* of the day stepping into a Mercedes SUV (Sport Utility Vehicle). After the refreshment, the Promotion Chief repeated a few key points to keep in mind, including the fact that we acted on behalf of the True Enlightenment Practitioners Association, and that our safety came ahead of everything else. This mission was to be carried out in a team, and each of the team's moves should follow the team leader's instructions. It was supposed to be a formal declaration on Buddhism to the public, a proclamation of what is actually right from wrong; it was going to be the Association's first step forward to uphold the true dharma as no other entity has done it

薩們聽課之用。我們也練習口號，並被告知警察最多舉牌三次，之後必得離開；為能互相照應，本車菩薩分為五隊，也配妥拉布條任務，大眾務必謹慎行事；每位菩薩沉默中流露著堅毅、果決。

過了新營 238 公里，得到的訊息是警察很多，到處都有。律師菩薩的手機從此不離耳朵，開始世間法上的張羅運作；推廣組長繼續洽詢細節，車內發放正覺背心，菩薩們掏出乾糧、喝飲料，車內逐漸活絡起來，頗有郊遊的生機。

抵達高雄巨蛋

八點三十五分聚集於公園邊小廣場，車腹中陸續撤下一箱箱宣傳單、標語、布條等；連同台中、台南來的同修們，加上高雄本地同修們共約四百來位菩薩；總指揮面授機宜，強調統一行動，同時間我們各自分發布條、標語，手攜正覺深藍背心；團隊並以台北南下三輛車共一百零三位菩薩為前鋒第一線。

背著朝陽，沿著綠林，一群靜默無聲，白色唐裝的隊伍，步履迅捷、穩實，隨著總指揮，邁向高雄巨蛋。

滿心跳躍的踩著行人道大步跨前，前進約五十公尺，聽得後面聲音雜沓；一轉身，看見數名揹有巨大相機的人員簇擁著誰；我們停下腳步，開始有人對話；忽聽得總指揮一聲：「拉開布條！」菩薩眾們旋即就地拉展，紛紛左右調適，拉出距離，也繼續挪往巨蛋正前方；瞧見斜前方有寬廣的左邊進場樓梯，一伸手拖住菩薩：「上梯子，站上去！」那【修雙身法的喇嘛教不是佛教】的布條就平地升起。

before in a thousand years' time.

Since his arrival in this land, the Dalai Lama had amended his itinerary a few times. He had cancelled a few activities, but there was still one morning gathering in the Kaohsiung Arena. If we were lucky enough, we would be able to get back in time to Taipei for the evening lesson given by the Head Master; in case we could not make it, there would be a DVD recording reserved for us. During the trip, we practiced our slogans and were informed that we would have to leave the site once the police had raised the offense signs for the third time. The members of my bus were divided into five groups. We were assigned the different banners-holding tasks and were told to be extremely cautious in every aspect. No remark was uttered among us. To be honest, we had no experience in this kind of endeavor, yet were well determined, as we clearly knew what we aimed to achieve. We were aware that this was only the starting episode.

Once our buses passed the point T238 Hsin Ying, we were informed that there were plenty of police around, nearly everywhere. One of the bodhisattvas in the group was a lawyer. He was eagerly making calls, maneuvering to get us an easier spot, or, perhaps a laxer police vigilance of the venue. The discussions between the frontier team and our bus became intensive: driving routes, entrance location, exit, etc. Each of us got a uniform vest to put on for later in action. We were getting closer by the minute. Some fished out biscuits, sandwiches and drinks; breakfast in the bus, together with the bright beaming morning sunshine and the wishful yet unpredictable program ahead of us, we felt as if we were going out on a field trip.

Arrival at the Kaohsiung Arena (Southern Taiwan)

Alongside the park square, boxes of brochures, banners and signboards were quickly hauled out from the buses to the sidewalk. We had just arrived in the vicinity of the Kaohsiung Arena; it was 08:35 a.m. There were around four hundred bodhisattvas altogether involved in this mission, including those from the regions of Taichung, Tainan and Kaohsiung. The team leader briefed us one final time on the tactic and re-emphasized the importance of working as a team. The banners and signboards were evenly distributed among us; everyone had the navy blue uniform vest ready in hand. It was decided that the hundred bodhisattvas from Taipei would be the front line demonstrators, a token of appreciation for our efforts for coming such a long way.

With the rising warm sun at the backs, the entire light-colored kung fu outfit group, led by the team leader, moved silently but briskly along the park lane towards the Arena. The on-looking green trees were quietly lined up, awaiting the scenario to come.

My joyously bumping heart nearly betrayed our grave mission. Striding forwards along the Arena block for about fifty meters, I heard some noise behind. I turned around, and unexpectedly caught the view of some weird shapes clustered together; someone was

又跑到年輕菩薩那條英文的【 *Lamaism, with the Couple-Practice Tantra, is not Buddhism！*】布條邊：「能站得上這兒嗎？」兩位年輕菩薩一屈膝，就躍上高架公園的邊緣，鮮黃底色的英文艷紅醒目句子：【*Lamaism, with the Couple-Practice Tantra, is not Buddhism！*】立即高高招搖於朝陽之下。「要站穩喔，注意安全！」只看見菩薩們報以微笑，點點頭。

當時只有一個作意，要讓群眾能清楚看見，也要讓媒體注意；又聽得：「穿上背心！」哎喲！忘了穿背心，我們又紛紛互助，握著布條、標語，同時穿上正覺的藍背心。

「**喇嘛教不是佛教！**」全體齊喊：「**喇嘛教不是佛教！**」

「**修雙身法的喇嘛教不是佛教！**」全體齊喊：「**修雙身法的喇嘛教不是佛教！**」這是跨入巨蛋範圍的第一次發聲。

巨蛋正前方整排行人道滿是黃布條及Ａ３標語與看板，這時，一群拿盾牌穿著藍灰警裝的警察蜂擁而出，一字排開，與巨蛋正前方站立的菩薩眾面面相覷，距離約一隻手臂長。

感覺汗水自頭頂泉湧而出；一群群即將入場的來賓走過巨蛋人行道，有人好奇轉頭看我們，有人目不斜視；正覺菩薩沉靜屹立，面容平和。

「要不要換手？」得到的答覆都是搖頭。

一位警察過來，為避免妨礙入場，請站立高架及階梯的菩薩下來；經過溝通無效，只能遵辦。

「喇嘛教根本不是佛教，卻以佛教的名義公開招搖撞騙；我

surrounded by several clumsy huge cameras. We stopped; I heard the sounds of a conversation. All of a sudden, a bare command, "**Pull the banners!**" Faster than anyone had realized, we were all gearing up for the big mission: adjusting the distance, stretching arms and straightening the banners. Our legs kept moving, the whole group kept advancing, approaching the front side of the Arena. At my left front, I saw a broad staircase leading to the left entrance of the Arena. My arms grabbed a bodhisattva, "**Up there, go! Get up the staircase!**" Up they went, and the bright yellow Chinese banner which read "*Lamaism, with the Couple-Practice Tantra, is not Buddhism!*" was hoisted upright aside the staircase.

I rushed to other young bodhisattvas, who were holding the English banner, pointed with my finger and asked, "**Could you manage to get up here?**" Without muttering a word, theirs knees tilted slightly, both of them hopped up to the edge of the artificial-sloped park. Again, the distinctly bright yellow banner which read the English words "*Lamaism, with the Couple-Practice Tantra, is not Buddhism!*" was unmistakably displayed under the morning sun.

"**Make sure you stand firm, safety first!**" They nodded and replied with broad smiles.

My sole intention at that instant was to draw attention by all means, either from the public or the media. "**Put on your vest!**" From somewhere came the order. Oh, we forgot our uniform. While still holding the banners or signboards, we helped each other, and within seconds, the navy blue vests were proudly shown.

"*The lamas' religion is not Buddhism!*"

"*The lamas' religion is not Buddhism!*"

We chanted the slogan.

"*Lamaism, with the Couple-Practice Tantra, is not Buddhism!*"

"*Lamaism, with the Couple-Practice Tantra, is not Buddhism!*"

Since we set foot in this region, it was the first statements that we made to the public, loud and clear.

The front sidewalk of the Arena block was entirely covered by a mass sea of yellow banners, signboards and A3 posters. Suddenly, a grayish blue shielded police troop, marching on the double, emerged from nowhere. They lined up straight ahead of the first-row demonstrators, face to face, in front of the Arena, so close that their badges were even within reach.

Even without much body motion, sweat trickled down from my head. As visitors walked past heading to the entrance, some curiously turned around and looked on, some unnaturally tramped forward like a robot. We stood still in silence, calm and composed.

"**Want a break?**" No one accepted my offer.

們只是正本清源，昭告大眾莫被誤導。」這位警察相當好奇也很友善，最後撤離時，也以宣傳單及《淺談達賴喇嘛的雙身法》與他結下正法緣。

這時於巨蛋正前方高處的樓梯，突然發出高聲吼叫：「政治迫害！政治迫害！」總共才五、六個人，迥異於我們群眾的靜默無語。

一位記者訪問發言人之後，耳邊聽得警察輕聲說：「可以走了吧？」

「走？你們要走嗎？」看他偏頭眯眯笑的臉，我直覺地問。

「是你們！」

這時，聽到我們「離開」的指令，轉身離去之前，掏出宣傳單與《淺談達賴喇嘛的雙身法》，就近遞給身邊幾位願意結緣的警察。這時聽見遠遠傳來一陣：

「喇嘛教不是佛教！」

「喇嘛教不是佛教！」

「修雙身法的喇嘛教不是佛教」……，

全身溼透黏答，熱烘烘的覺受，內心卻是清朗乾爽。

回到公園，更加的口乾舌燥，菩薩們互相遞上講堂備妥的杯水、飲料還有扇子。方才沉寂挺立堅忍無畏的悍士，變成眼前調柔軟語的菩薩；綠葉、木凳，飲水、抹汗，觸目有志一同的道侶；清風不解世間愁，若有還無任戲遊。所謂有因有緣世間集，共此良辰吉時，莫非是承接三百多年前辯經後的泥濘之戰？緣於 平實導師深妙證

An officer approached me, telling me that the bodhisattvas standing next to the entrance and on the edge of the high-sloped park ought to be removed in order not to obstruct the entrance of the Arena. After my failed negotiations, we had to obey and withdraw.

"From the very start, the religion of the lamas has had nothing to do with Buddhism, yet they have been exploiting the faith and dedication of Buddhists worldwide to enrich their own interests. We, as the true Buddhists, are obliged to make the actual facts known to the society. Their plots must be stopped; the public must not be misled anymore." The officer was rather friendly, and curious as well, so I told him about our mission. Later on, at our withdrawal, I did offer him a publication from our association called *Decoding the Dalai Lama's Copulation Tantra Practice* and some of our brochures. This way, he could have some positive link with the Buddha dharma in the future.

"Political oppression! Political oppression!"

All of a sudden, a violent bellow burst out from the upper part of the staircase. I searched round for the noise, and spotted around five or six unknown individuals clustered together. What a big contrast in number and sound volume in comparison with our unit.

After our spokesperson granted an interview to a reporter, I heard a police officer whisper in my ear, **"Ready to go?"**

"Go? Are your troops leaving?" Looking at this officer's smiling face, I asked bluntly.

"No, it's you!"

Simultaneously I heard the **"Depart!"** instruction shouted by the team leader. Before my departure, I quickly handed out a couple of brochures and a few copies of *Decoding the Dalai Lama's Copulation Tantra Practice* to the police officers around me who were willing to accept. This simple act would enable them to have a connection with the Buddha dharma, if not in this life, maybe in a future life. Meanwhile, a gentle chanting in the distance could be heard,

"The lamas' religion is not Buddhism!"

"The lamas' religion is not Buddhism!"

"Lamaism, with the Couple-Practice Tantra, is not Buddhism!"…

From top to toes, I was drenched in sweat, I felt the heat, but my mind remained lucid and tranquil.

Once we were back to the park, I enjoyed the delightful bottle of water and the fan handed to me by other members to quench my thirst and heat. The then-solid, perseverant warriors had turned into every amiable, kind bodhisattvas. Within views there were green leaves, stools, drinks and sweat, which mingled with the dharma companions who shared common goals; I could feel the breeze of the innocent wind which was playful with or without

量，夜以繼日奮筆疾書勝妙法義之辨證書籍，揭示當代佛教聞所未聞知見，開演不可思議如來妙法接引有緣；佐以同修們奮力推廣正覺書刊，摧邪顯正利樂有情；同心教化社會大眾，共同培植福德，使正法之威德力日益增強；並仰賴佛力、願力、因緣業力，方得成就此時重燃戰火卻無須短兵相搏，使泥濘轉炎陽，由隱闇趨向光明、大眾化！

主力戰

於地上完成沙盤演練，總指揮等站起身，重新整隊布署巨蛋疏散出口處人員位置，以紅綠燈十字街角為重點位置。第一隊已出發，第二隊在公園街角，一輛警車幾乎駛上人行道。

警察所長開口：「你們修明心見性，人人各有因緣，為什麼要攻擊別人？」所長真是做了功課，他又一次重複強調「明心見性」。

「我們不是來說『明心見性』，我們來指出喇嘛教不是佛教，不可欺瞞大眾，誤導佛教徒！」

「你們集眾聚會，待會兒媒體過來又要舉牌，這是我的轄區，我必須負責。」

「那媒體未來之前，我們靜靜站立又沒聲音，可以聚集囉？」我不放棄。

律師菩薩過來溝通，發現早上運作的範圍是巨蛋的對區；此處隔一條馬路，咫尺天涯沒有世間人情。我不再多說，決定離開，到對街馬路人行道。近午炎陽毫不留情，果真等施無差別。走到對街，

Spring.

As it is said in Buddhism, there are causes and karmas behind every gathering; nothing is coincidental. Could this be the sequential battle of the one that took place three hundred years ago after the two parties' formal dharma authentication debates, when we were forced by the defeated yet more powerful party into a muddy fight in Tibet? Nowadays, due to our Venerable Master Pings' marvelous level of realization, we can benefit from his numerous comprehensive books which refute non-Buddhist teachings and from his lessons, which explain in great details the profound true dharmas, unheard of in contemporary Buddhism, and which aim to bring in those inclined towards Buddhism. In addition, the bodhisattvas of the True Enlightenment Practitioners Association aim to spread our publications widely, and vow to expel false teachings out from true Buddhism, with a view to benefit all Buddhist followers. This mission was exactly an educational occasion for the society to witness the true dharma, an occasion for us to accumulate merits and virtues together. As a result, the power and glory of the true dharma will certainly strengthen. This initial crusade was made possible by the Buddha's blessings, our vows and the karmic powers of causes and conditions. Nevertheless, we did not need to engage into hand-in-hand fights in muddy darkness the way we did in the past; we now aim to move forward to counter our rivals under the bright sunlight and openly in the public.

Main Battle

The team leader rearranged the tactical dispatches after mapping out the plan on the park's ground. The traffic light intersections outside the Arena exits were the focal locations. Team One had already set off. Team Two was just around the corner of the park, as a police car pulled right up to the pavement.

"**Your school focuses on cultivation for enlightenment and seeing the Buddha-nature. But everyone has got his own karmas and goals; why do you have to attack the others?**" The Chief Officer spoke straight to the point; he repeated the words "enlightenment" and "seeing the Buddha-nature."

"**We are not here to propagate 'enlightenment and how to see the Buddha-nature'; we are here to point out the fact that the lamas' religion is not real Buddhism; they should not fool people and mislead Buddhists!**"

"**You group has assembled a huge crowd within my control area; when the media show up, you will certainly raise your protest signboards, and I am responsible for this area.**"

"**But if we stand here quietly until the media show up, then are we allowed to remain here?**" I tried.

一位師兄指著前方：「師姊到那邊！」我疑惑的看著他，「那邊可以遮太陽！」

仍是上班時間，車輛不多，身旁菩薩手錶顯示十一點四十分，我們蓄勢等待巨蛋散場，正覺菩薩們布滿巨蛋周邊十字街口。

不久，看見本條街口的師兄們穿上背心，不放心地跑去確認，已見他們拉開黃色布條沿街站立，人人各就各位；果然行人逐漸增多，也開始有摩托車來回。八線道馬路對面散場的參與密宗法會人士，一群群緩緩沿道而行，大部分的頭臉不可避免地望向我們的布條；車輛越來越多，騎士越來越密集，車行減緩，看見騎士嘴唇唸著：**「修雙身法的喇嘛教不是佛教！」**

看哪看！人人都在看，已經種下正法的種子，未來只待時節因緣！數百年的等待，就在此時此刻；烤爐似的炎陽，讓我們體溫高升，血液也逐漸沸騰！

面前大遊覽車、人群、摩托車，擠成一團。身後人行道也有好奇的人群，轉身微笑趨前結緣；對方說：「妳們跟喇嘛有過節嗎？」她謹慎的問。

「不是過節，由於喇嘛教不是佛教，卻以佛教之名誤導佛教徒，詳情請看這個。」便把手中的宣傳單及《淺談達賴喇嘛的雙身法》遞給她，她點點頭收下。

「甚麼是『雙身法』？」過來一位中年人問；

「對！問的好，請參考這個真實的內容，仔細看喔！」

「妳們怎麼用『淫』這種字眼？佛教怎麼用這樣的字眼？」

The lawyer came over to communicate with the Chief Officer; we soon found out that this area was under the jurisdiction of another police officer, different from the one who looked after the area opposite the traffic light and whom we spent time in the morning building a relationship with. I decided not to waste any second here, walked across the avenue with the others. We were all baking in the generous southern Taiwan sunlight. One brother member pointed to the front and said to me, "**Sister, over there!**" I looked at him puzzlingly. "**Over there, you can stay in the shade!**"

It was still office hours, not much traffic was to be seen. The wristwatch belonging to the companion next to me read 11:40 a.m. We were waiting with full anticipation for the program in the Arena to end. All members were squarely dispatched all around the intersections.

Soon enough, I saw brother members put on their uniform vests at the far end of our block; I hurried over to make sure their action was agreeable with the timing. Within seconds, banners and signboards were amply raised to their parade position. The avenue regained live with pedestrians and motorcyclists within views. Attendees of the Dalai Lama gathering exited in groups on the other side of the eight-lined avenue, walking leisurely right opposite us. We were much too obvious to be ignored by any pairs of eyes. The avenue was gradually occupied by cars and motorcycles; I could clearly see a motorcyclist mouth the words written on our banners, "***Lamaism, with the Couple-Practice Tantra, is not Buddhism!***"

Take a look, here! Everyone was watching; the seeds of the true dharma had already been sown onto the lookers-on. Only timing and karmas were needed to bring forth the corresponding occurrences in the future. After several hundred years of waiting, this was the very moment. Our body temperature was heated up by the scorching sun; I felt my heart pounding!

Touring buses, crowds and motorcycles were jam-packed right under my nose; behind us were also curious pedestrians, I turned around to answer their enquiries. "**What's up between you and the lamas?**" A lady asked cautiously.

"**It's nothing personal. The religion of the lamas has nothing to do with Buddhism at all, yet they have covered themselves up as Buddhists and have misled Buddhist followers all along. Have a good look here for more details.**" I handed her a copy of *Decoding the Dalai Lama's Copulation Tantra Practice* and some leaflets, while she nodded in agreement.

"**What is 'Copulation Tantra' after all?**" A middle-aged man inquired.

"**Good question! Please check out these; they will tell you the actual facts.**"

"**How could you have such 'obscene' wordings in your text? Buddhists are not supposed to express themselves in such a way.**" Another one disagreed with a deep frown to show his discontent.

另一位皺著眉頭的路人，很不滿意。

　　「是嘛！簡直離譜到不可想像，卻又是事實，才不得不寫出來啊！所以一定要看這份資料，我們敢印出來就要負責，請參考！」也遞上一份宣傳單及《淺談達賴喇嘛的雙身法》，他雖然嘀咕，倒也沒有拒絕。

　　這時候三位青壯喇嘛經過，一位手裡還捏著我們的宣傳單，我趨前問：「能看中文嗎？」

　　「這是哪裡？」正在講手機略說中文的那位喇嘛問我。我仰頭找路牌，他竟把手機塞給我！

　　「……這裡是巨蛋斜前方的十字路口，……中國石油，忠誠路……，……Joy Plaza 前面……」我向遊覽車小姐解釋半天，顯然她的車子也是外地進城；我請三位在這個定點等，車子會來接他們，我又建議他們到 Joy Plaza 大樓陰影處候車，不必站在這兒烤太陽。三位迷途羔羊離去時，路邊拉布條的一位師兄轉過身，遠遠地向我豎起拇指。

　　結束後回公園接過便當，坐下用餐，方覺腳底及腳邊痠痛，扶著木桌坐下。享用便當時，徐風撫過，眼前樹葉可以如此青綠，還貼心的遮擋炎陽；木條椅、泥土香、小樹叢還有螞蟻，才想起，幾千個日子不曾參加郊遊野餐了？周邊菩薩們的燦然巧笑，溫言輕語：「那三個喇嘛要作甚麼？」

　　「妳（你）們注意到啦？」

　　「當然囉！安全問題啊！」

"Certainly not. It's utterly beyond anyone's imagination, yet those are the actual facts; it's also the reason we ought to speak out the truth! Anyway, you must take a good look at these materials. We know what we are doing, and are fully responsible for our deeds. Please do refer to these!" I also handed him some materials. He was still mumbling, but at least did not reject me.

At the same moment, three young lamas appeared, one of them holding our green leaflet in his right hand. I recognized it instantly and stepped forward to ask him, "**Can you read Chinese?**"

"**Where are we now?**" The other one who was on the mobile asked me directly. I looked around, as a stranger here as well, trying to locate our position. Abruptly, he pushed his mobile into my hand!

I tried to explain our location to the tour guide on the other end of the mobile, "…**Right in front of the Arena, at the intersection slightly towards…, a China Petroleum Station, Chung Cheng Road…, …yes, in front of the Joy Plaza…**" Obviously, she was a visitor to this city too, so I spent a lot of time explaining our location. I told the lamas to wait at this spot for their touring bus to collect them. Also, seeing the blazing sunlight right atop their bare heads, I suggested that they wait in the shade of the Joy Plaza Building. A brother member who was holding one side of the banner at a distance turned to me with one thumb up, as the three lost lambs walked away from me.

Once we were back to the park and were offered with a lunch box each, I leaned against the wooden table, and then noticed my yelling sore feet.

While munching my food, I enjoyed the gentle breeze of the wind, noticing that tree leaves could have incredibly various tones of green to cope with the burning heat. The wooden bench, the scent of the earth, the bushes and the crawling ants. … It suddenly hit me, how many thousand days had gone by since I last had my picnic in a garden? I heard some tender voices, accompanied by radiant smiles. "**What did they want, those three lamas?**"

"**You did notice?**"

"**Sure thing! Security matters!**"

"**They lost their way, which was only a tiny loss compared to a much bigger one – their ignorance regarding the truth of life!**"

Indeed, what a unique, luxurious feast.

Two thousand and five hundred years ago, Demon Mara impudently hastened the Buddha to enter the nirvana state; what was then his backbone to support this intrusive courage? Demon Mara knew well enough, as long as the true dharma remained unknown to the public, all sentient beings would certainly stay connected to the states that appeal to the

「這是他們的小迷啊！嚴重的大迷還沒指點哪！」

是喔！多麼奢侈的午宴啊！

二千五百年前，天魔仰仗何種聲勢，膽敢親自催促 世尊早入涅槃？天魔深知，只要正法實義晦暗不明，眾生必然執取意識相應境界，欣樂五欲流轉生死，輕易地任由天魔操弄於股掌之間。自古以來，喇嘛教竟然匪夷所思，利用佛法名相，裹以「密」字糖衣蠱惑天下，世人趨之若鶩，尤以權貴為盛；今日的我們，意欲連根斬除千年以降盤根錯節、根深柢固的聚魔窟；正邪深戰伊始，披荊斬棘，困頓危阨也是意料中事。

以「正覺風」標顯警世清流之第一役，如同芝蘭入於鮑魚之肆；五濁世間習以麤重取勝，五、六人的咋呼嘶吼，媒體大力報導抗議衝突，有意無意亦將正覺扯入嗆聲衝突事件中，完全背離事實真相。眾生看佛，佛是眾生；顛倒日久，何以強求？

想當初，若沒有 平實導師挺身而出，力挽狂瀾，你我可能已經走在馬路的另一邊參加密宗祈福灌頂；眼前，若沒有正覺這一次以及未來無數次堅毅卻震撼的機會教育，我們的眷屬子孫以及自己的未來世，全將成為虎口羔羊而讓天魔額手稱慶。忍不住又想起那三位羔羊，他們原可以是真正的佛弟子，或是 平實導師珍愛的小金獅。正覺菩薩眾既然走入正法之門，讓我們與無量無數的有緣眾生，把握契機共同成就於人間最具足的一切種子的智慧，也不枉過去無量世所經歷的生死與宿願！謹以此文供養正覺菩薩團，法眷屬原本是患難與共，同圓佛菩提！

謹以一偈作結：

conscious mind. They would indulge in sensual desires and would be trapped into the endless rounds of births and deaths *(samsara)*. This way, they would all be herded into Demon Mara's kingdom. Since its inception, the lama's religion has been using the Buddhist terminology in an abusive way, sugar-coating their teachings with a "Secret" flavor, and actually replacing the essence of practices with the lamas' own inventions. They have managed to fool the entire world up to this day. Their followers join their movement in a swarm, led by influential celebrities. This trend has prevailed in a deep-rooted and interlocked way for more than a thousand years, but we are determined to destroy the den of demons. This is just the beginning of a crusade of the right to eradicate the evil. Of course, we are mindful of the challenges and perils that will obstruct our path as we head towards our goal.

Our initial crusade was performed in the "True Enlightenment" style, which stood for serenity and a clear warning to the society. Comparatively speaking, it was like a mild fragrance pervading the smelly fish market. It was only natural to draw the public's attention using a violent way of expression in this mundane world. The bellowing of the five, six persons in the morning was later broadly reported by the media in the evening news. Worst of all, the news put the focus on the strong conflicts among the demonstrators outside the Arena, more or less implying that we were involved in some violent clash. That was entirely untrue. As the Buddhist saying goes, "From an ordinary mortal's eyes, the Buddha is but an ordinary man; but from the Buddha's eyes, an ordinary mortal is precisely a Buddha." This is the way things are in the world!

To begin with, if the Venerable Master Pings did not courageously stand up to the evil, misleading lama's religion, with his dharma wisdom and righteous mind, you and I might have been on the other side of the avenue attending the Dalai Lama's gathering. Moreover, without the True Enlightenment Practitioners Association giving the society a shocking and overwhelming lesson via this mission and the many more to come, our family members, children and ourselves in future lives will all turn into Demon Mara's herds, to his biggest delight. I could not help thinking of those three innocent lamas, who lost their way after the gathering. They could have been disciples of the true Buddha dharma, or the Venerable Master Pings' precious golden-hair lion cubs (outstanding enlightened students). As the True Enlightenment bodhisattvas who have entered the true dharma door, let us make the best out of our blessed opportunities, together with countless sentient beings, to accomplish the all-seed-wisdom, for which one has the full potential in this human realm. In such a way, our vows and the uncountable rounds of births and deaths that we spent pursuing the ultimate truth during our past lives would not have been wasted. With my heartfelt sincerity, I humbly submit this article to the True Enlightenment bodhisattvas as a footnote to the initial crusade. Once in the dharma door, we are supposed to work together and attain Buddhahood through thick and thin!

A closing *gatha*:

重燃聖戰正覺子，旋乾轉坤除魔害；
泥濘推趨炎炎日，不盡有爲續法脈。

南無本師　釋迦牟尼佛

南無極樂世界　阿彌陀佛

南無當來下生　彌勒尊佛

南無　文殊師利法王子

南無　觀世音菩薩摩訶薩

南無護法　韋陀尊天菩薩摩訶薩

南無　克勤圓悟菩薩摩訶薩

南無　玄奘菩薩摩訶薩

南無　平實菩薩摩訶薩

南無正覺親教師菩薩摩訶薩

南無正覺海會菩薩摩訶薩

菩薩戒子　正子　合十謹誌

二〇〇九年九月六日

The true Buddha's sons have re-kindled the holy crusade,
Worth turning the Earth to eliminate Demon Mara's deeds;
Murky combats progressed toward open glowing encounters,
The true dharma lineage will continue to be carried out in the world.

Namo Original Teacher Buddha Sakyamuni

Namo Buddha Amitabha of the Pure Land

Namo Forthcoming Buddha Maitreya

Namo Dharma Prince Manjusri

Namo Bodhisattva-Mahasattva Avalokitesvara

Namo Dharma-Protecting Bodhisattva-Mahasattva Skanda

Namo Bodhisattva-Mahasattva Profound King

Namo Bodhisattva-Mahasattva Xuan Zang

Namo Bodhisattva-Mahasattva Pings

Namo Bodhisattva-Mahasattva Direct Dharma Teachers of the True Enlightenment

Namo Bodhisattva-Mahasattva Practitioners of the True Enlightenment

Bodhisattva Precepts Holder
Zheng Zi, with joint palms
September 6, 2009

2009/09/01 高雄活動紀實

Kaohsiung Activity Records, September 1, 2009

2009/9/2 旺報 A2 版報導：
2009 年 9 月 1 日高雄市／達賴喇嘛 1 日在高雄巨蛋舉行祈福法會，
上百位正覺教育基金會成員在會場外表達抗議。（謝明祚攝）

September 2, 2009, News report from Page A2, Want Daily:
September 1, 2009, Kaohsiung / The Dalai Lama held a prayer ceremony in the
Kaohsiung Arena. Over a hundred members of the True Enlightenment Education
Foundation staged a protest outside the Arena. (Photograph by Xie Mingzuo)

2009/9/2 中國時報 A4 版報導：
2009 年 9 月 1 日高雄市／約 400 位正覺教育基金會的成員拉起黃布條抗議，抗議達賴的修雙身法非佛教正法。（周敏煌攝）

September 2, 2009, News report from Page A4, China Times:
September 1, 2009, Kaohsiung / About four hundred members of the True Enlightenment Education Foundation displayed the yellow banners, protesting that the Couple-Practice Tantra propagated by the Dalai Lama is not a true Buddhist dharma. (Photograph by Zhou Minhuang)

以上活動照片──摘錄自 TVBS 新聞台。
The above activity photos are retrieved from TVBS News.

此一活動照片──摘錄自東森新聞台。
This activity photo is retrieved from ET News.

修雙身法的密宗喇嘛教不是佛教！

Lamaism, with the Couple-Practice Tantra, is not Buddhism!

修雙身法的密宗喇嘛教不是佛教！

Lamaism, with the Couple-Practice Tantra, is not Buddhism!

正覺菩薩們為護眾生挺身而出，呼籲大眾了知達賴喇嘛祈福無效、所募善款應留給災民。

To protect the sentient beings, the True Enlightenment bodhisattvas stepped forward and made a public request: People should know that the Dalai Lama's prayer is ineffective and the entire donation should be given to the victims of the disaster.

喇嘛與女信徒合修的雙身法，絕對不是佛教中的修行方法，是從印度教性力派引入喇嘛教中，違背佛教正法的教理與修行法門。達賴喇嘛為首的藏傳「佛教」實質上只是喇嘛教，根本不是佛教。喇嘛教的無上瑜伽、樂空雙運是輪座雜交、師徒亂倫、破壞家庭的邪淫法，只會戕害學佛人造下邪淫破戒的大惡業，修密的女人使家中丈夫被偷戴了綠帽子，死後會下墮地獄受苦無量。知道內情的佛弟子應該指出其外道邪淫的本質，將此入竄佛教的外道喇嘛教逐出佛教之外，避免有人繼續受害。

The couple-practice of copulation by the lamas and the female followers is absolutely not the Buddhist practice method. The couple-practice of copulation was introduced from the Hindu Tantrism into Lamaism, which violates the correct Buddhist doctrine and dharma-gate of practice. Tibetan "Buddhism," led by the Dalai Lama, is only Lamaism in essence and is not Buddhism at all. Lamaistic the Highest Yoga Tantra (the Dual Operations of Bliss and Emptiness) is an evil and licentious dharma that involves changing partner during the couple-practice of copulation with multiple partners as well as having sexual relationship between teacher and disciple, and it will also destroy family. It makes the Buddhist learners create a severe evil karma of adultery that breaks the precepts. While alive, a Tantric female practitioner will make her husband wear a green hat. After death, she will unavoidably fall into the hell realm with immeasurable sufferings. Those Buddhists who know the truth should point out its evil and licentious nature of non-Buddhism. The non-Buddhist Lamaism should be expelled from Buddhism so that people will not become victims again.

花絮一：在活動其中有人用極度粗魯的方式對和平的女性抗議者近距離拍攝，帶有恐嚇意味，絕非文明人應有的行為。

Titbit of information 1: During activity, someone was taking a close photo of a female peace protester in an extremely rude way, with a threatening attitude. It is not a proper behavior that a civilized person should have.

花絮二：這本來是一個單純的宗教宣示及社會教育活動，卻因爲
這位有政治意圖人士極端無理行爲，以臉部特寫的近距離方式對
平和的女性宣示者拍攝特寫，加上各種言語挑釁，使單純的宗教
宣示活動被強行染上政治色彩。把宗教活動扭曲爲政治活動，顯
然不是一個有教養的文明人應有之行爲。

Titbit of information 2: Originally, it is only a simple religious declaration and social educational activity. However, this man, with political intent, was taking a close photo of the face of a female peace demonstrator, and giving verbal offence. Because of his extremely rude behavior, the simple activity of religious declaration is polluted with political intention. Distorting a religious activity and making it become a political one is obviously not a proper behavior that a civilized person should have.

花絮三：2009/09/01 約 11 時 35 分許，在高雄巨蛋綜合體育館對街，突然出現一位身穿紅衣的台籍喇嘛，以極端粗鄙淫穢的言語向我們侮辱，甚至毀損我們的宣傳文宣；正覺菩薩從地上撿起被他搶去揉成一團的文宣品，平和地繼續宣示；一次又一次，始終沉默而以慈悲心態面對他的叫囂。

Titbit of information 3: September 1, 2009, around 11:35 a.m., across the street from the Kaohsiung Arena, a Taiwanese lama in red suddenly appeared and verbally insulted us with extremely rude and obscene words; he even tore our leaflets to shreds. The True Enlightenment bodhisattvas picked up the crumpled leaflet, which was snatched and dumped to the ground by him, and continued the peaceful demonstration; again and again, the True Enlightenment bodhisattvas always faced the situation with silence, looking upon his shout with compassion.

花絮四：紅衣喇嘛政治栽贓說：什麼達賴喇嘛邪淫下地獄？你們是毀謗，是國民黨的爪耙子！

Titbit of information 4: For a political set-up, the lama in red said, "Are you saying that the Dalai Lama commits adultery and will fall into the hell realm? This is slander. You are the informers of Kuomintang (KMT)!"

上圖乃是密宗的雙身像，女性最後都要與喇嘛這樣合修。

The above picture is a couple-body statue. Eventually, the women will have the couple-practice of copulation with lamas like this.

附錄二、達賴來台祈福的真相

　　2009 年的南台灣，8 月 8 日暗夜的超級颱風造成大水災，冤枉死了許多人，當台灣南北所有民眾都忙著救濟事宜時，達賴卻藉機前來台灣造勢宣傳密宗的法義。達賴喇嘛此次來台灣，表面上的名目是風災災民的祈福法會，其實是在狂賺災難財；暗中的目的只是爲了鞏固密宗在台灣各處設立的道場，以便繼續廣傳雙身法，支持所有喇嘛們繼續與密宗女信徒合修雙身法，名之爲慈悲與博愛。

　　但因爲受到廣大民眾的唾棄，也因爲輿論的激烈反對，所以這回達賴的藏獨政治秀便收斂起來，只是繼續假冒爲觀世音菩薩的化身，依舊身穿紅衣來支持密宗喇嘛們繼續在台灣搞男女雙修法，美其名爲「藏傳佛教」。然而若是探究達賴的本質，他藉著風災祈福的名義前來台灣，只是藉著南台灣災民的苦難來作秀，他這回所有的開支都是由台灣百姓來買單的，無形中使得原本應該用在救災的資源，轉而被用在此達賴祈福的事件上面，使災民應該獲得的救濟物資暗地裡減少了。

　　話說回來，台灣有一個名人出了許多錢財，請達賴來台爲災民祈福消災，其實是很冤枉的；因爲花了那麼多錢財請來達賴祈福消災，事實上卻是完全無福而且一點點的災也消不掉的，只是又再一次從台灣獲得大量的資財，帶回達蘭莎拉的流亡政府，用來大力搞藏獨；也藉著達賴來台，爲台灣的密宗各道場壯大聲勢，想要達到擴大信眾的目的，藉以挽回因爲正覺同修會的破斥而流失的密宗群眾，才能使達賴的經濟來源鞏固不失。

　　然而達賴這回來台的目的如果成功了，就表示又會有更多的台灣女性被喇嘛所迷惑，於是繼續走上與喇嘛合修雙身法的邪路，紅

Appendix B Truth of the Dalai Lama's Visit to Taiwan for Prayer

On the night of August 8, 2009, the super typhoon caused the large floods and many people died. When all Taiwanese people were busy with the disaster relief, the Dalai Lama took the chance visiting Taiwan to advertise his Tantric doctrines. Under the guise of praying for the victims but in fact earning the disaster money, his another hidden purpose is to consolidate the cultivation centers in Taiwan so that the lamas can widely propagate the Couple-Practice Tantra; he supports the lamas to continuously cultivate the Couple-Practice Tantra with their female believers and dignifies it with the name of compassion and love for all.

Due to the strong public opposition, the Dalai Lama does not make a political show of Tibetan independence this time, but disguises himself as the reincarnation of Bodhisattva Avalokitesvara and supports the lamas in their continuous practice of the Couple-Practice Tantra in Taiwan; he dignifies his religion under the name of "Tibetan Buddhism." However, concerning his intention of this Taiwan visit, the Dalai Lama is only coming here for making a show in the name of prayer for the victims, and Taiwan people pay all the expense of his visit. Those resources, which should be used for the disaster relief originally, have been shifted to his prayer activities, indirectly resulting in the decrease of the resources for the victims.

In Taiwan, a famous person made a significant donation to invite the Dalai Lama for prayer. It is in fact not worthwhile to spend so much money because the Dalai Lama's prayer is totally ineffective in relieving the victims and has no merits at all. It can only enable him to bring a huge amount of money from Taiwan back to the exiled government in Dharamsala to support Tibetan independence, and increase the number of believers in the cultivation centers all around Taiwan in order to compensate for the decrease of believers and money, which results from the refutation by the True Enlightenment Practitioners Association.

If the Dalai Lama's purpose of this visit were achieved, it would mean that more Taiwanese females would be seduced by the lamas, continue cultivating the evil Couple-Practice Tantra with them, commit the hell karma of sexual misconduct, and fall into the evil paths after death with the lamas. As to the husbands of those female believers, they would be inevitably cuckolded (being forced to wear a green hat) in secret. Therefore, in this Taiwan visit, the Dalai Lama not only took advantage of the

杏出牆而犯下邪淫的地獄業；捨壽以後不免雙雙淪墜，而修學密宗的台灣女性家裡的丈夫們，可就難免被暗中戴上了綠帽子。所以這回達賴喇嘛來台，不僅是災民被消費了，還要讓台灣男人戴綠帽子。男女合修的雙身法—密宗喇嘛與女信徒上床交合—本來就是密宗的根本教義，這就是密宗法義與實修上的本質。也就是說，密宗的本質完全是依著男女交合中的性高潮來建立教義的，假借佛教修證的種種名詞，而以喇嘛與女信徒上床交合所獲得的樂觸來取代，自始至終都與佛教的斷我見、斷我執、斷世間執著、證悟明心、眼見佛性、成就實相智慧完全無關，而且完全是意識的境界。

　　密宗的「修證」自始至終都是意識境界，而意識已是生滅法，不是常住不壞的金剛法，所以他們號稱的金剛乘—以喇嘛的性器官在長時間交合中保持堅挺不軟而名為金剛—所以自稱是金剛乘，其實從來都不是 釋迦牟尼佛所說的金剛法如來藏心。釋迦佛說的金剛法是第八識心如來藏性如金剛，世間永無一法可以用來摧折或毀壞如來藏心，所以如來藏心名為金剛心。大家熟知的《金剛經》就是在講解這個金剛心，所以才名為《金剛經》。但密宗喇嘛們所傳的金剛法，只是經由中脈明點的觀想，氣功的鍛鍊、盤腿跳躍的鍛鍊、性器官的鍛鍊，來達成性器官的堅挺不軟而假名為金剛法，與佛教法義中所說的金剛心如來藏完全無關，所以根本就不是佛教。縱使他們能練成性器官始終堅挺不軟、永不洩精，而能連續幾天與幾十位密宗女信徒輪座雜交，終究還是生滅性的意識境界，與佛法中說的金剛法如來藏心的實證無關，依舊是生滅法而不是《金剛經》所說的金剛法。所以密宗根本沒資格自稱金剛乘，所修所證全都是意識境界，而意識卻只能存在一世，每一世的意識都是全新的，所以每一個人入胎出生以後都不知道前世的事情。

disaster victims but also made the Taiwanese men wearing a green hat. The couple-practice of copulation between the Tantric lama and his female follower is essentially the root doctrine of Tantric practice; it is the essence of Tantric doctrines and actual practice. That is to say, the doctrines of Tantric practice are based on the orgasm of copulation; it replaces the different Buddhist realization levels with various kinds of tactile happiness obtained from the couple-practice of copulation between the lamas and their female followers. All those kinds of happiness are the states of conscious mind and completely have nothing to do with the eliminations of self-view, self-attachment and worldly attachments in Buddhist practice; it also has nothing to do with the Buddhist attainments of enlightenment, seeing the Buddha-nature and the wisdom of the ultimate reality.

All Tantric "practices and realizations" belong to the states of mind-consciousness, which is the arising-and-ceasing dharma rather than the *vajra* (diamond) dharma, which is everlasting and indestructible. However, the Tantric practitioners refer to maintaining a stiff erection for quite a long time during copulation as the *vajra* dharma and call their practice *vajra-vehicle* (*vajrayana*). It is in fact never the *vajra* dharma of the Tathagatagarbha mind that the Buddha preached. What the Buddha said about the *vajra* dharma means that the characteristic of the eighth consciousness Tathagatagarbha is like a diamond (*vajra*), and there is nothing in the world that can damage or destroy Tathagatagarbha. Therefore the Tathagatagarbha mind is named the *vajra* mind. The well-known *Diamond Sutra* is exactly the discourse on this *vajra* mind and thus named. Nevertheless, the *vajra* practices propagated by the lamas are the visualization of bright-drop in the central channel, Chi-Practice, jumping with a cross-legged posture, and the exercise of sexual organ so that they can have a stiff erection for a long time. Those practices have completely nothing to do with the *vajra* mind Tathagatagarbha in Buddhist doctrines and are by no means Buddhism. Even the lamas can, after long time practice, get a stiff erection without ejaculation for several days and have sex with several tens of female believers in turn, it is still within the scope of the arising-and-ceasing conscious mind and totally irrelevant to the actual realization of *vajra* dharma Tathagatagarbha. It is still the arising-and-ceasing dharma, but not the *vajra* dharma expounded in the *Diamond Sutra*. The Tantric practice can never be qualified as *vajra-vehicle* because what they realize are all the states of mind-consciousness, and the conscious mind can only exist within a lifetime; every conscious mind of each lifetime is totally new; therefore, everyone cannot know anything about his past lives.

　　達賴喇嘛所率領的密宗喇嘛們，把與女信徒暗中交合，幫助女信徒達到性高潮的閨房淫樂技藝，美其名爲無上瑜伽，是假冒佛教出離生死的實證名相；這些喇嘛們在台灣乃至全球各地，都是這樣假冒佛教的名義來爲女信徒廣做祕密灌頂。女信徒被做了祕密灌頂以後，心就歸屬於喇嘛了，自然就全心全力爲喇嘛們辯護說：「我們密宗沒有男女雙身法，我們從來沒聽說過喇嘛有傳雙身法。」然而密宗神秘兮兮的號稱密宗，其實就是因爲這種與女信徒祕密交合的教義不許公開，所以才被稱也自稱爲密宗的。這是密宗的所有喇嘛們都無法否認的事實，也是密宗喇嘛達賴的創派祖師宗喀巴所寫的《菩提道次第廣論》的〈止觀〉之中所說的教義內容，更是他所寫的《密宗道次第廣論》中所公開講說的教義內容，誰也無法否認。如果他們否定了雙身法、捨棄了雙身法，密宗就不再是密宗了。

　　若論密宗的本質，最後可不是女信徒一人與喇嘛暗中交合了，而是要有許多密宗女信徒與喇嘛同在密壇中輪座雜交的；這樣一來，當然是喇嘛們身穿紅衣而女信徒們的丈夫都同樣被戴上了綠帽子。偈曰：

> 老千凱子來組合，上師明妃性交合，
> 你在旁邊送鈔票，鞏固頭上大綠帽。

　　因爲密宗的弘傳，本質上是千年大老千的世間最大謊言，假借佛教的名義來欺騙信徒，把所有信徒都當作無知的凱子。所有密宗女信徒的丈夫們努力賺錢來給妻子修學密宗，而妻子卻是常常與密宗喇嘛暗地裡上床合修雙身法，這個雙身法所證得的樂空雙運境界卻與佛法的實證完全無關；丈夫們卻繼續支持妻子學密，支持妻子繼續與喇嘛常常上床合修雙身法，這不是天下最大的凱子嗎？

　　學密的女人總是幫著喇嘛們辯解說：「我們密宗從來都沒有雙身

The Tantric lamas, led by the Dalai Lama, dignify the obscene skills about helping the female believers reach the orgasm through copulation with the name of the Highest Yoga Tantra; they steal the Buddhist realization terms, which are for the liberation from births and deaths. These lamas, whether in Taiwan or all over the world, extensively make the secret empowerment for the female believers like this way with Buddhist terms. Once empowered in secret, these female followers obey the lamas and defend them with all their hearts: "The Tantric practice does not have the Couple-Practice Tantra for the male and female; we have never heard that the lamas propagate the Couple-Practice Tantra." However, the reason why the Tantric practice is so secretive is in fact that this kind of copulation with female follower cannot be allowed in public. This is the fact that all Tantric lamas cannot deny. It is the doctrine of the chapter "Samatha and Vipassana (Tranquility and Insight)" in *The Great Treatise on the Stages of the Path to Enlightenment (LamRim)* of Tsongkhapa, who is the founder of the Dalai Lama's Gelug Sect. The Couple-Practice Tantra is also a teaching given publicly by Tsongkhapa in *Extended Treatise on the Progression of the Esoteric Path* and cannot be denied. If they negate the Couple-Practice Tantra and abandon it, the Tantric school will not be the Tantric school any more.

As for the essence of Tantric practice, not only one but many female believers are required to have sex with the same lama in turn at the altar in the final stage of practice. Therefore, the lamas, in red robes, make those husbands of the female followers wear a green hat (cuckolding those husbands). The verse states:

The swindler and the fool get together; the teacher and the female consort have sex together. You stand aside, donate money, and wear a big green hat on your head.

The propagation of Tibetan Buddhism is essentially the greatest lie in the world by the great millennial swindlers, cheating the believers in the name of Buddhism and treating them as the fools. All husbands of those female believers work hard and earn money to let their wives learn Tantric practice; however, their wives cultivate the Couple-Practice Tantra in secret with the lamas and obtain the state of the Dual Operations of Bliss and Emptiness, which have totally nothing to do with the realization of the Buddha dharma. Those husbands continue supporting their wives to frequently have sex with the lamas through the Couple-Practice Tantra; aren't they the most foolish in this world?

Many female Tantric practitioners will defend the lamas by saying: "Tibetan

法，我們跟隨的喇嘛從來沒有教我們雙身法。」這樣的說法是可以諒解的，因爲如果承認了，就等於承認自己紅杏出牆的事實了，豈不是要與家裡的丈夫正式鬧翻？所以一切已經與喇嘛上床合修過雙身法的密宗女信徒，當然要爲喇嘛們辯護。但是卻又常常在密宗的佛堂中合搞雙修法，她們家中全無所知的丈夫們，還自以爲是男子漢，卻還在鼎力支持心愛的妻子與喇嘛學密——幫助妻子常常在密宗佛堂中與喇嘛們合修雙身法。這其實是引狼入室的行爲，因此而造成學密女性家庭中，夫離子散的情況；而這些悲慘事件一籮筐又一籮筐，可是爲了保護女性的名節所以大多私了，被披露出來的永遠都只是冰山的一角，於是喇嘛們就可以繼續矇騙密宗女信徒的丈夫們。

　　所有密宗女信徒的丈夫們的頭上，全都有這個綠帽疑雲——**我心愛的妻子是否已經與喇嘛們上過床了？我現在還來得及阻止她們的第一次嗎？**因此，所有密宗女信徒的丈夫們都應該及早加以釐清，千萬別讓枕邊人上當了還以爲是在佛法中有所實證。如果您心愛的妻子已經與喇嘛上過床了，而妻子卻還以您辛苦賺來的錢財供養喇嘛，那麼這與消費星期五餐廳的午夜牛郎有什麼不同？只是堂而皇之假借學佛之名作爲掩護，而可以常常和密宗喇嘛交合，獲得性滿足罷了！

　　騙財騙色的密宗仁波切，全都是欺世盜名的假慈悲者；達賴喇嘛率領著所有喇嘛們，每天口中都高唱「博愛」的口號，其實是要愛盡天下所有的女人—要與天下所有女人都一一交合—要使天下所有女人都因爲喇嘛而獲得性高潮，前提是這些女人都必須年輕而有姿色。達賴喇嘛又常常高喊著「慈悲」，本質還是要使天下所有女人都能在喇嘛們的胯下獲得性滿足，美其名爲「慈悲」。這才是密宗喇嘛教所說「博愛」與「慈悲」的眞實意思。

Buddhism does not have the Couple-Practice Tantra; the lama whom we follow does not teach us the Couple-Practice Tantra." We can understand the reason why they say so; if they admit the existence of the Couple-Practice Tantra, it means they admit their sexual misconduct at the same time; that will result in a broken marriage with their husbands. Therefore, all those females who have cultivated the Couple-Practice Tantra with the lamas will defend the lamas. Although the female Tantric practitioners cultivate the Couple-Practice Tantra in the Tantric temple hall frequently, their husbands do not know the reality at all and still support their wives, whom they love so much, to have the couple-practice of copulation with the lamas in the temple hall. This behavior hurts them very much because it will destroy the whole family. Such miserable things happen again and again; only very few cases are disclosed out of the consideration for the females' reputation. Consequently, the lamas can continue to cheat those husbands whose wives cultivate the Tantric practice.

All the husbands of the female Tantric believers have a doubt about whether they are wearing a green hat: **Has my beloved wife made love with the *lama*? Is it still in time for me to stop her first sexual misconduct with the *lama*?** Hence, all husbands of the female Tantric believers should understand the true facts as sooner as possible, and never let your wives be deceived with a misconception that they have actual realization in the Buddha dharma. If your beloved wife have had sex with the lama and she still offer the money that you earn hard to the lama, it is similar to pay a gigolo for sex. The only difference is that she copulates with the lama and gets the sexual satisfaction, but covers her behavior under the name of Buddhist practice.

All Tantric *rinpoches* who deceive people for both money and sex are the fake compassionate who get their fame by cheating. The Dalai Lama and his lamas promote the slogan of "love for all" everyday, and their intention is in fact to make love with all women in the whole world—to let all of them have the orgasm through copulating with the lamas. The slogan "compassion" which the Dalai Lama frequently says is essentially to let the worldwide women have the sexual satisfaction from between the *lama's* thighs, in the dignified name of "compassion." This is the real meaning of "love for all" and "compassion" in the Tantric Lamaism.

Under the guise of Buddhism, the Dalai Lama teaches the lamas to have a real practice of sexual misconduct. Led by the Dalai Lama, Tibetan Buddhism gets lots of money from Taiwan and widely performs its political show all over the world in the dignified name of "peace, love for all and compassion," but is actually a greatest

　　達賴喇嘛假佛教的名義，教導所有喇嘛們真行邪淫；而密宗正是以達賴喇嘛為首，從台灣獲得錢財，廣在全球遍搞政治秀，頂著「和平、博愛、慈悲」的光環，暗地裡卻是天下最大的騙子。喇嘛們在台灣要吃、要錢、要女人，達賴喇嘛幫助這些喇嘛們達到目的，而台灣喇嘛們就每年出錢供養達賴喇嘛，密宗就在達賴與喇嘛們互助之下共榮起來了。然而這全都是由憨厚的台灣男人買單。

　　達賴率領前來台灣的喇嘛們，這樣子騙盡台灣男人的善心及錢財；心裡還不滿足，這次還要假借八八水災前來台灣，為南台灣的受災民眾作無效的祈福；其實是假借水災來欺騙台灣民眾，藉機再撈一筆不義之財，同時鞏固台灣密宗喇嘛教的勢力，保護達賴未來繼續在全球搞藏獨時最大財源的台灣密宗。

　　台灣島上的所有丈夫們都要有自我認知：只要妻子開始學密了，自己就隨時都有可能成為綠帽子的擁有者。而密宗女信徒一旦開始跟隨喇嘛學密了，遲早都會走上雙身法的路子—只在於時間的早晚差別—沒有不與喇嘛上床合修雙身法的，因為密宗的「密」就是指雙身法；所以密宗女信徒的丈夫們，遲早都會被戴上綠帽子。這是密宗女信徒的所有丈夫們都難免的宿命，除非這些丈夫們的妻子既醜又沒錢財供養喇嘛。如果長得不醜，或者有許多錢財供養喇嘛，她的丈夫就難免有被戴綠帽的危機。

　　所有台灣男人乃至全球的男人，務必要認清喇嘛教：密宗之所以自稱為密宗，之所以被認定為密宗，全都是因為祕密而不可說出來的雙身法所致。所以您的妻子若已經與喇嘛合修了雙身法，當然是絕對不會承認的。您若是對密宗認識不清楚，或是妻子否認有學雙身法以後，就同意妻子繼續學密，那麼：性侵春風吹又生，紅袍之下頂綠帽。您將暗中被「加冕」！

swindler in the world. The lamas in Taiwan want food, money and women; the Dalai Lama helps them achieve these objectives, and the lamas donate money to the Dalai Lama every year in return. Tibetan Buddhism flourishes under the cooperation between the Dalai Lama and his lamas, with donations from homely, simple Taiwanese men.

In such a way, the Dalai Lama and his lamas take advantage of Taiwanese men's kindness and cheat them out of all their money. But the Dalai Lama is still not satisfied and came again to perform an useless prayer ceremony for the typhoon victims in southern Taiwan, with the hidden purposes of collecting money from Taiwanese people again and consolidating the influential power of Tantric Lamaism in Taiwan so that the lamas can make sure that Taiwan, their biggest fund provider, will continue to support his worldwide activities of Tibetan independence.

All husbands in Taiwan should have the following self-awareness: Once their wives start to learn the Tantric practice, they themselves might become the green hat wearers anytime. Since the core doctrine of Tibetan Buddhism is the Couple-Practice Tantra, if the females start to learn the Tantric practice with lamas, they will cultivate the Couple-Practice Tantra of copulation with them sooner or later, without any exception. Therefore, those husbands of female Tantric believers will be cuckolded eventually. This is the inevitable fate of those husbands except their wives are ugly, and they themselves are poor. Otherwise, they will be under the risk of wearing a green hat.

All men in Taiwan or even in the whole world should clearly understand the following facts about Lamaism: The reason why Tibetan Buddhism is so secretive is because the core doctrine, the Couple-Practice Tantra, is secret and cannot be disclosed. Hence if your wife has practiced the Couple-Practice Tantra with the lama, she will never admit it. If you do not understand Tibetan Buddhism, and agree that your wife can keep on learning the Tantric practice after her denial of the Couple-Practice Tantra, **the sexual assault will happen again, and you will wear a green hat secretly given by the lama in red robes.**

There are lots of sexual assaults caused by the lamas. Once they are disclosed, their formal statement is that those lamas are fake lamas but not the formal ones in their system. But once those lamas are identified as the formal ones in their system, their formal statement will change and become that the lama with sexual assault is only an isolated incident, whereas all the other lamas are not involved at all. About

　　密宗喇嘛們惹出來的性醜聞非常多，一旦出事了就說那個喇嘛是假喇嘛；若是被拆穿眞喇嘛的身分時，就推說那只是偶發事件，宣稱其餘喇嘛都不是這樣的。然而吾人不免頌云：

　　　　無獨有偶頻頻出，報章雜誌皆可稽；
　　　　神秘喇嘛教底細，實乃性力雙修法。

　　　　眞假喇嘛皆雙修，謊稱秘密來灌頂，
　　　　若騙不成強性侵。

　　　　混入正統佛教中，假名藏傳之佛教，
　　　　千年世紀大騙局，消費雪域之藏民；
　　　　今逢寶島災難時，騙局又在台灣演；
　　　　達賴來台之紀實，性交謊言兼斂財；
　　　　凡是台灣大丈夫，不可不知此眞相。

　　　　藏傳佛教喇嘛教，達賴祈福寫眞集，
　　　　紅衣綠帽性醜聞，曠古迄今最大宗；

　　　　詐騙集團最大宗，超過千年之騙局；
　　　　號稱無上瑜伽法，淫亂人妻稱佛法。

　　　　自身邪淫死下墮，來世人身自不保；
　　　　諸佛早已斥爲魔，全無修證眞外道；

　　　　自身福德已銷盡，諸佛皆摒非佛子；
　　　　美名祈福之法會，諸佛不祐祈無用。

　　密宗喇嘛們其實都是神棍，在達賴喇嘛的率領下，以佛教外表及佛法名詞作包裝，並且還號稱是比佛教的 釋迦牟尼佛證量更高；這樣貶抑 釋迦牟尼佛的騙子，竟然還敢向 釋迦牟尼佛祈求保祐，說穿了只是一群經過千年設計出來的斂金術罷了。所有聰明人深入

these, the following verses state:

> Lots of cases have been disclosed, with the reports from the newspapers or magazines; the real fact of the secret Lamaism is in fact the sexual Couple-Practice Tantra.

> Both the true and fake lamas cultivate the Couple-Practice Tantra, with the lie of secret empowerment. If they cannot seduce the females, they will rape them instead.

> They sneak into the true Buddhist system and use the deceiving name of Tibetan Buddhism; it is in fact a millennial fraud, and the Tibetan people are exploited. Now they take the chance of disaster and play fraud in Taiwan again. The facts of the Dalai Lama's visit are sex, lie, and money fraud. All Taiwanese husbands should know this truth; the truth of Tibetan Buddhism, Lamaism, or the Dalai Lama's prayer is the sex scandals about the lamas in red robes and the green hats of those husbands. The sex scandals of the lamas have been the most serious ones from the ancient time till now.

> They are the biggest cheating group, and it is a fraud over a millennium; they claim it is the Highest Yoga Tantra, and yet they copulate with others' wives in the name of the Buddha dharma.

> They commit the sexual misconduct and will fall into the evil paths after death, losing their human bodies in the next life. All Buddhas refute and call them the demons who have no practice realization and are actually the non-Buddhists. They have used up their welfare and merit, and all Buddhas exclude them from being the Buddha's sons.

> Although they dignify it with the name of praying ceremony, it is useless since all Buddhas do not bless them.

The lamas of Tibetan Buddhism are in fact the religious swindlers; led by the Dalai Lama, they advertise themselves with the Buddhist appearance and terms, and even claim that their realization level is much higher than that of Buddha Sakyamuni. Surprisingly, such swindlers who slander the Buddha dare to request Buddha Sakyamuni for blessing. It is actually a well-designed millennial fraud for money. After carefully thought, all the wise will know their lies and frauds, and will not be deceived. Only those who are ignorant and superstitious will be fooled.

上圖是密宗喇嘛教雙身「佛像」，是男女雙修的性交圖；若那個與喇嘛性交女
性是您的家人，您將情何以堪？

The above picture is the couple-body "buddha statue" of Tantric Lamaism, a picture of the couple-practice of copulation. If the woman copulating with a lama is your family member, how can you endure this?

想一想就知道他們的謊言與騙局了，如何還肯上當呢？只有愚癡而迷信的人才會上當。

如今這個千年騙術的謎底，早已經被人具體舉證拆穿了！（詳見《狂密與眞密》總共四輯書中的全面舉例辨正。）而喇嘛教的所有教義也都與佛法無關，因爲他們把所有佛法全面加以變造，本質都是外道的意識境界法，而且是印度教中的性力派閨房技藝，與佛法完全無關。如果學佛的女性受了五戒、比丘戒、比丘尼戒、菩薩戒以後，與喇嘛上床合修了雙身法，或者受戒以後的男性與女上師或密宗女行者合修了雙身法，都是犯了邪淫罪中的最重罪；依據佛戒，死後都會下墮無間地獄中。這樣教人邪淫犯罪而且自己也在實行雙身法而犯下邪淫罪的達賴喇嘛，連自己都救不了，何況能爲南台灣的同胞們祈福？未之有也！

密宗的無上瑜伽，說穿了就是與喇嘛交合的享樂法門；女性修學密宗以後，早晚都必須要與喇嘛上床合修雙身法，達到遍身快樂的意識境界，美其名爲成就報身佛果，其實只是密宗自創的「抱身佛」罷了，都與佛法無關。而且實修了以後，除了破戒以外，同時也成就了破壞 釋迦牟尼佛正法的破法者；所以密宗的教義其實是失靈了的羅盤，已經是航向地獄的指針。

密宗的教義本是惑人的宗教騙局，他們是組織性的犯罪者；藉著佛教的名義亂扯一番，也能騙到成爲世界性的宗教；洋人只要一提到佛教就認爲是密宗，然後佛教就被冤枉成常常在歐美犯下性侵害的案件的宗教了。

年輕人若剛好值遇情路不順時，往往被不知情的迷信者轉介而去找喇嘛，想要改運、求得好運；或者正好遇到生意上有障礙而不

Now the millennial fraud has been disclosed and refuted with real evidence. (Please refer to the arguments and refutations in *The Wanton versus True Secret Schools,* four volumes.) Actually all doctrines of Lamaism have totally nothing to do with the Buddha dharma; they completely change the Buddha dharma into the non-Buddhist dharma belonging to the state of mind-consciousness, with the essence of sexual skills from Hindu Tantrism. If a female Buddhist who has accepted the Five Precepts, Bhiksuni Precepts or Bodhisattva Precepts cultivates the Couple-Practice Tantra with the lama, or if the male who has accepted the precepts cultivates the Couple-Practice Tantra with the female guru or practitioner, she or he will commit the gravest sin of sexual misconduct. According to the Buddha's precepts, she or he will fall down into the un-intermittent hell after death. The Dalai Lama, who teaches others to commit the sin of sexual misconduct and commits the sin as well by himself, cannot save even himself, not to mention praying for the people in southern Taiwan; it is impossible!

The Highest Yoga Tantra of Tibetan Buddhism is simply the method of enjoying sex with the *lama*; after learning the Tantric practice, the females will cultivate the Couple-Practice Tantra with the lamas sooner or later and attain the state of mind-consciousness with the whole-body bliss, which is dignified with the name of reward-body buddha fruition. This kind of fruition is created by them and irrelevant to the Buddha dharma. Once having had a real practice, they will break the precepts as well as destroy the true dharma of Buddha Sakyamuni; thus, the doctrines of Tibetan Buddhism are in fact like a malfunctioned compass, always pointing to the hell.

The doctrines of Tibetan Buddhism are essentially the religious fraud that cheats people; they are the well-organized criminals who cheat others under the guise of Buddhism and make Tibetan Buddhism become a worldwide religion. The Westerners have always regarded Tibetan Buddhism as Buddhism, and wrongly think that Buddhism is related to the sexual assaults in the western countries, which are in fact committed by the lamas of Tibetan Buddhism.

For those youths who are frustrated in love and referred to the lamas for good luck by someone who is ignorant and superstitious, or those who face obstacle on their business and are referred to the lamas for good luck, although they become the Tantric practitioners for the pursuit of luck, they should be careful about the following:

如意時，被轉介去找喇嘛求好運，成爲密宗信徒。然而要小心的是：

　　　本求好運變好孕，男獻鈔票兼妻女；
　　　女則獻身供上師，改運脫衣兼脫褲；

　　　無效就說心不誠，說妳上供錢不夠；
　　　加碼奉上大紅包，方得上師來灌頂。

　　　矇著丈夫受密灌，珠胎已結喇嘛子；
　　　如是好運成好孕，返家大讚密宗好；

　　　丈夫戴著大綠帽，還讚喇嘛眞神奇；
　　　於是奉上大紅包，感謝喇嘛成好孕。

　　達賴喇嘛暗中實行雙身法，書中也公開承認了；然而達賴一族修得都是抱身佛，絕對不是報身佛，與佛教修證全然無關，正是以李代桃僵的手法眞正破壞佛教正法的人。密宗的祈福、慈悲、博愛的秘密，其實就是以出家人的身分廣受供養，同時又可以擁有在家人的淫樂，根本不是佛教、不是佛法，卻欺騙世人說他們是最究竟的佛教正法；而達賴喇嘛正是這群世紀大騙局的詐騙集團首領。

　　喇嘛教密宗的修行，必須有女人交合取得淫液，才能作爲密灌中的甘露。而達賴喇嘛率領的喇嘛教，基本教義就是男女交合的雙身法，最後的第四灌還必須有許多女人與喇嘛們輪座雜交的。這就是宗喀巴的性修書《菩提道次第廣論、密宗道次第廣論》中所說的止觀修法。不幸的是現在已經有不少佛教寺院淪陷了，所以在信受密宗而修學密法的佛教寺院中，每夜總是淫聲喧騰，只是寺外虔誠的信徒們聽不到罷了！所以，受不了誘惑，偶爾犯下邪淫戒的僧人並不是破壞佛教最嚴重的人，密宗才是最嚴重破壞佛教的人；因爲密宗是以外道性交的雙身法來公然取代佛教正法的，也是明著鼓勵

The pursuit of luck ends up with the pregnancy in return; the males offer their money, wives and daughters; the females offer their bodies to their gurus and take off their clothes and pants to change their lucks; if it does not work, the lamas will make the excuse that you are not sincere because you have not made enough offerings. Even you offer more money and get the empowerment from the guru finally, the result is that the female has obtained the secret empowerment without the acknowledgement of her husband and gotten pregnant with the *lama*; she will praise the Tantric practice for the transformation from luck to pregnancy; but the poor husband will be forced to wear a green hat; he even admires the miracle of Tibetan Buddhism and offers huge sums of money for his wife's pregnancy by the *lama*.

The Dalai Lama cultivates the Couple-Practice Tantra in secret and publicly admits it in his books. What they have achieved in Tantric practice are the embracing-body buddhas and have completely nothing to do with Buddhism; they destroy the true Buddha dharma through replacing the right with the false. The secret of the Tantric prayer, compassion and love for all is in fact receiving offerings with the monastic appearance and enjoying the sexual happiness of lay practitioners at the same time. They are neither the true Buddhists nor the teachers of the Buddha dharma, but they pretend that their religion is the ultimate, true Buddhism. The Dalai Lama is exactly the leader of this great, millennial, fraudulent group.

In the Tantric practice of Lamaism, the nectar of secret empowerment comes from the obscene liquid of copulation. The fundamental doctrine of Lamaism is the couple-practice of copulation, and its fourth empowerment of the last stage must be performed by the lama copulating with many females in turn. This is the content of Samatha and Vipassana practice mentioned in Tsongkhapa's sexual practice books, *The Great Treatise on the Stages of the Path to Enlightenment (LamRim)* and *Extended Treatise on the Progression of the Esoteric Path* (or called *Great Exposition of Tantra*). Unfortunately, many Buddhist monasteries have been changed into Tibetan Buddhism; there are sexual activities taking place every night in those monasteries, but the pious believers outside the monasteries do not know the truth at all. The monks who occasionally violate the precept of celibacy in secret are not those who destroy Buddhism the most; the lamas of Tibetan Buddhism are the ones who destroy Buddhism the most because they publicly replace the true Buddha dharma with the evil non-Buddhist Couple-Practice Tantra. Lamaism is an evil religion that

佛教僧人精修雙身法的邪教，達賴喇嘛正是這群嚴重破壞正法的密宗首領。邀請這樣破壞佛教正法的人來台灣，能向 釋迦牟尼佛祈福嗎？能爲南台灣的民眾帶來幸福嗎？

　　密宗喇嘛的邪淫事實，說出來眞的很難令人相信；然而事實擺在眼前，卻又令人不得不信。頌曰：

> 達賴始祖宗喀巴，著作性侵財色書：
> 菩提道次第廣論、密宗道次第廣論。
> 專弘密宗雙身法，依教奉行喇嘛教，
> 背後眞相知多少？密宗勇父明妃合，
> 密壇淫合晝夜修，極盡情慾非佛法，
> 修雙身法非佛教。
>
> 藏密雙修方便法，上師喇嘛尋佛母，
> 精挑細選要年輕，美貌純眞又姣好；
> 人老珠黃喇嘛嫌，即須多財大供養，
> 方能擁抱喇嘛身，同入密壇共愛樂。
>
> 喇嘛若住貧窮處，人煙稀少無少女，
> 老女醜女可充飢；若實無女畜生可，
> 母豬亦能賽貂蟬；只要全身遍樂已，
> 便說已成報身佛。
>
> 達賴等眾來台灣，咬住無知金龜婿；
> 給你精液名甘露，淫害大眾羞羞修！
> 喇嘛專挑你妻女，少女熟女有錢婦，
> 全部都可當佛母。若是年輕又貌美，
> 姿色身材樣樣好，首選具相之明妃，
> 一切喇嘛心傾倒，無財亦可不計較。

encourages the Buddhist monks to diligently cultivate the Couple-Practice Tantra, and the Dalai Lama is exactly the leader of this religion that seriously damages the true dharma of Buddhism. It is useless to invite such a person who destroys the true Buddhism to Taiwan for prayer; how can Buddha Sakyamuni bless him? How can Taiwanese people get the blessing from the Buddha?

It is unbelievable that the Tantric lamas have committed so much obscene sexual misconduct. However, according to the disclosed facts, we cannot but believe it. The following verses states the facts:

> Tsongkhapa, who is the founder of the Dalai Lama's Gelug Sect, wrote the following books about sexual assault, money fraud and sex: *The Great Treatise on the Stages of the Path to Enlightenment* and *Extended Treatise on the Progression of the Esoteric Path*. Those books especially propagate the Couple-Practice Tantra and teach the Tantric practice of Lamaism. What is the real truth behind it? Both the male and female Tantric consorts copulate together; they have obscene sex every night at the altar and extremely enjoy the sexual happiness, which are not the Buddha dharma at all. The Couple-Practice Tantra is not Buddhism.

> In the Couple-Practice Tantra, the guru looks for the buddha-mother, who must be young, beautiful and pure; if she is old and ugly but wants to co-practice with the lama, she must offer lots of money so that she can have sex with him and enjoy the sexual happiness.

> If the lama lives in a poor place where there is no girl, he can have sex with the old or ugly women. If even the old or ugly women are not available, he can have sex with the female animal as well; he can treat the female pig as a beautiful girl; after enjoying the whole-body bliss, he claims that he has become the reward-body buddha.

> The Dalai Lama and his followers come to Taiwan to cheat the ignorant, rich husbands; they give you the nectar, which is actually semen, and hurt people through the obscene Tantric practice! The lamas select your wife, your daughters, young girls, mature women or rich women as their buddha-mothers. Those girls who are young and beautiful with a good figure are the best candidates for the female consorts, and they are the best lovers for all lamas. If you are poor and ugly, the lamas will not be happy to have you as their female consort.

年輕貌美有姿色，即是喇嘛最心愛；
若妳沒錢兼很醜，他不樂妳當明妃。

台灣男人當留心：家中女眷學密後，
不久您就戴綠帽；愛妻失身您失財，
大把鈔票往上供；當了龜公須保密，
只為顧及妻名節。家中妻女學密後，
男人眼淚暗中滴，有苦難言向誰訴？
喇嘛讓你戴綠帽，你上供養當凱子，
豈非天下最冤枉？學密女性之丈夫，
賠了夫人又折兵；綠帽蓋頂難離身，
暗虧受了有誰知？

喝酒吃肉又性侵，喇嘛雜交染性病；
哪天妻子被傳染，丈夫不久也上身。
台灣男人當認清：喇嘛陽具名金剛，
自妻女陰是蓮花，金剛蓮花互相入，
號稱方便加智慧；若探喇嘛房門內，
男女合抱正在修，無上灌頂大手印，
名為樂空之雙運，期望彼女非汝妻，
無異緣木而求魚。

喇嘛性愛的枷鎖，第一堂課是供養，
最後一堂必性交，合修當然是汝妻。
此乃無上瑜伽灌，陰陽合體之雙修，
密宗最高之密法，用下半身性器修。
你獻妻女當供養，妻成智慧實體印，
此印活佛懷中坐，上師懷春抱你妻；
臉紅春盪無上樂，邪淫亂倫雜交合，

The Taiwanese men should be careful: If your wife learns the Tantric practice, your will be cuckolded soon; your beloved wife loses her chastity, and you lose money; with huge money as the offering, you have been cuckolded but should keep it secret in order to protect your wife's reputation. If a wife learns the Tantric practice, her husband will weep in secret and cannot complain at all.

It is extremely unfair that the lama makes you wear a green hat but you donate money to him like a fool. For those husbands whose wives learning the Tantric practice, they lose both their wives and money; the green hat is put on their head, and they cannot get rid of it; no one knows the suffering except them.

The lamas have alcoholic drink, eat meat and make the sexual assaults; they have sex with many women and thus might get the venereal disease. In case the wife is infected, the husband will get the disease soon. Taiwanese men should know: the *lama's* penis is called *vajra*; the pudendum of your wife or daughter is called lotus; the penetration of the *vajra* into the lotus is called expediency and wisdom; the lama and woman embracing together to practice the unsurpassed empowerment method of Mahamudra in the house is called the Dual Operations of Bliss and Emptiness; it is impossible to expect that the female is not your wife or daughter.

About the trick of the lama's sexual teaching, the first course is offering, and the last one will be copulation, with your wife as the sexual mate. This is the empowerment of the Highest Yoga Tantra, the couple practice of both male and female bodies. The highest secret method of Tantric practice is cultivated using the sex organ of the lower body. If you donate your wife as the offering, she will become the Wisdom Seal of real body; this seal sit on the living-buddha, and the guru embrace your wife for sex; enjoying the sexual happiness with a blushing face, they perform the obscene copulation in turn and lie that it is the great practice of Buddhism, but in fact they have submitted the application for the hell. If your wife gets close to the lama, you will be cuckolded.

Now we disclose the great millennial trick as well as the secret in the altar; the meaning of love for all and the lama's prayer is to have sex with all women in the world; even the female animals are used as well,

謊稱佛教修大法，實寫地獄申請書。
汝妻若與喇嘛近，外遇綠帽必蓋頂。

今揭千年大騙局，又揭壇城下秘密，
博愛祈福諸喇嘛，淫遍全球諸女人；
母畜一樣不放過，色情片商嘆不如。

紅色外衣和平獎，博愛天下之女人；
桃色陷阱要小心，別讓妻子變佛母。
喇嘛床上之性奴，密壇性交的祭祀，
淫火灌頂之法會，汝妻只是消耗品。

騙財騙色全記錄，就是密宗喇嘛教！
千年神棍大集團，惑人咒術加政爭；
邀請達賴來祈福，請鬼抓藥真愚癡，
飲鴆止渴是傻瓜。

還請認清喇嘛教，專贈綠帽給男人；
遠離綠帽護家人，全家都應離密宗。
喇嘛邪淫真面目，世人不知又迷信；
邪淫喇嘛遍地有，吹噓誇大的證量；
實乃貪淫的淫蟲，淫盡天下人妻女。
遵奉宗喀巴教導，喇嘛佛母淫合修，
號稱最高的證量，十六小時淫不停。
本屬謊言大籠罩，假冒佛教之令名，
美名藏傳之佛教，千年附佛大騙局。
實非佛教假名稱，同名佛教不同質；
西藏密宗真相貌，如今藏不住秘密。
性侵謊言加斂財，就是喇嘛真面目。

and it is far more disgusting than the pornography.

With the red robes and Nobel Peace Prize, his love for all is loving all women in the world; everyone should be careful about the love trap and do not let your wife become buddha-mother; don't let her become the sexual slave of the lama and the victim of copulation in the altar. Your wife is only a sacrificial offering in the dharma ceremony of the empowerment with obscene desire.

All records of the Tantric Lamaism are about deceiving people for both money and sex; the lamas are the great millennial fraud group involving deception, sorcery and political fight. Inviting the Dalai Lama for prayer is as stupid as drinking poison to quench thirst.

Everyone should know that Lamaism makes the husbands wear a green hat; in order to avoid that, we should keep ourselves far away from Tibetan Buddhism. The lamas are in fact obscene, but people are ignorant and superstitious; those obscene lamas exist everywhere; they boast and exaggerate their realization level but are exactly the greedy satyrs who want to have sex with others' wives and daughters. Following the teachings of Tsongkhapa, the lamas and buddha-mothers copulate to cultivate the Couple-Practice Tantra; the highest realization level is continuously having sex for sixteen hours. It is essentially the biggest lie with Buddhist terms. They dignify it with the name of Tibetan Buddhism, but it is actually a millennial trick in the guise of Buddhism. They are by no means Buddhism; although in the name of Buddhism, the essence of Tibetan Buddhism is completely different from the true Buddhism. The real face of Tibetan Buddhism cannot be kept secret now; sexual assault, lie and money fraud are the true face of the lamas. Please protect your family so that your wife will not commit sexual misconduct; please also understand Tibetan Buddhism and stay away from the possibility of a green hat.

We must terminate the lie of Lamaism, which is in fact a group of satyrs with Buddhist clothes.

The top mountain of snow area in Lamaism is imagined as the Buddha land of Shambhala or called Shangri-La; they think it is the pure land of human world. With the apotheosized story in movie, they deceive people with the dignified lies; the real fact is that their practice is just a very

還請保護您家人，以免紅杏出牆圍。

認清密宗綠帽廠，遠離密宗綠帽雲。
終結喇嘛教謊言，披著袈裟的色狼。
雪域之巔喇嘛教，幻想香巴拉佛土；
又傳香格里拉名，號稱人間之淨土。
配合電影神格化，美麗謊言唬世人；
實則低級雜交配，假佛教名騙千年。

活佛上師仁波切，吹噓證量比佛高；
名為密宗抱身佛，外披紅衣內色狼；
佔盡便宜還賣乖，斂財性侵搞政爭；
祈福晃子綠帽實，斂財更分化種族。

八八水災能滅村，密宗喇嘛能滅族：
引來鬼神常擾亂，諸佛不祐天災頻。
你獻妻女及金錢，喇嘛為你戴綠帽；
吾人苦心揭穿它，無奈依舊有人迷。
家有女眷學密者，必修喇嘛雙身法；
非唯送您綠帽戴，妻女亦恐地獄招。
若請喇嘛進家門，色狼就在您身邊；
堂而皇之淫您妻，外帶勾引您女兒。
吃肉喝酒助淫興，號稱無上瑜伽密；
若信密宗之信徒，最終宿命必雙修。

紅衣喇嘛之狼吻，男失妻財女失身；
學密灌頂搞輪座，淫人妻女騙錢財。
無上瑜伽即性交，師徒亂倫雜交配；
屎尿淫液加腦髓，名為五種甘露飲。

low-level partner-changing copulation; Lamaism disguises itself as Buddhism and has deceived people for a millennium.

All living-buddhas, gurus and *rinpoches* boast that their realization level is higher than that of the Buddha and call the realization the Tantric embracing-body buddha. They are all the satyrs in red robes; they take all the benefits but are still not satisfied; therefore they devote themselves to getting money, sexual assault and political fight. Prayer is only an excuse and giving green hat is the fact; in addition to getting money, they also disunite people.

The typhoon disaster can ruin the village, but the Tantric lamas can ruin the whole race. They beckon the ghosts to disturb people; therefore, all Buddhas do not bless people, and disasters happen frequently. You donate your wife, daughter and money, but the lama makes you wear a green hat in return. We painstakingly disclose it, but unfortunately some people are still seduced. The female family members who learn the Tantric practice will cultivate the Couple-Practice Tantra with the *lamas* eventually. Not only you are cuckolded, but also your wife and daughters will fall down into the hell. If you invite the lama to your house, the satyr is just beside you; the lama will directly have sex with your wife as well as your daughters. By eating meat and drinking alcohol to enhance the sexual happiness, the lama calls this practice as the secret Highest Yoga Tantra; the believers of Tibetan Buddhism will cultivate the Couple-Practice Tantra finally.

The satyr kiss of the red-clothed lama will make a male lose his wife and money, or make a female lose her chastity; the *lamas* teach Tantric practice with the empowerment of partner-changing copulations, having sex with others' wives and daughters, and cheating others for money. The Highest Yoga Tantra is in fact the partner-changing copulations between teacher and disciples. Feces, urine, obscene fluids and brain are called the five kinds of nectar.

The wise, rational Taiwanese people should calmly observe that all the lamas' diligent practices of stiff erection, including the Mahamudra performed by the male and female consorts together as well as the absorption of vital energy from the female, are not the Buddha dharma at all. The truth of sexual misconduct in Tibetan Buddhism is seducing

這是藏傳「佛教」立姿雙身法的「佛像」，密宗喇嘛、仁波切，他們與您的妻子就這樣暗中合修無上瑜伽、樂空雙運。

This is the couple-body "buddha statue" of Tibetan "Buddhism" in standing posture. The Tantric lamas or *rinpoches* are privately doing the couple-practice of the Highest Yoga Tantra (the Dual Operations of Bliss and Emptiness) with your wife like this.

有智理性台灣人，冷看喇嘛勤勃起；
勇父度母大手印，御女採氣非佛法。
密宗邪淫之眞相，嬲亂女性壞家風；
紅袍下之春夢揚，情慾追求世間樂；
卻假聖人尊貴名，欺矇世人號活佛。
藏密最高的法門，密續無上瑜伽法，
實是邪淫雙身法；喇嘛灌頂與香妃，
甘露淫液的來源；光怪陸離是密宗，
邪淫達人活佛們；外現賢良和平使，
內懷貪淫搞性侵；博愛背後之目的，
愛盡天下諸女人；引入密壇密灌後，
上師弟子搞亂倫；專用下半身修行，
大費功夫使勁修；即是喇嘛邪淫法，
此乃佛誡所不許！

活佛假借宗教名，政客喇嘛來祈福，
小心是禍不是福。唸唸有辭勾招咒，
滿嘴消災及解厄；身現祈福心淫聲，
政治伴奏斂財秀。吃盡抹乾吹牛王，
明說爲民消災厄，暗搞錢財和美色。
喝酒吃肉玩女人，透視藏密喇嘛教；
雙身修法之面目，密宗永遠難否認。
性交酒肉及醜聞，桃色法會之性奴；
紅白菩提雙修出，男女行淫之淫液，
號稱明點甘露丸，不外糞尿及淫液。
頭蓋骨與人皮鼓，污穢不堪之法器；
兩眼睞女上下觀，空行金剛蓮花密；

the female and destroying the good family practice.

The spring dream is fulfilled under the red robes, and the worldly happiness of sexual desire is satisfied; however, under the guise of holy saints, they deceive people in the name of living-buddha.

The highest practice method of Tibetan Buddhism, the Tantric Highest Yoga Tantra, is actually the obscene Couple-Practice Tantra; the empowerment by the lama with the female consort is the source of the obscene fluid, the nectar. The Tantric practice is wicked and strange. Those evil, obscene living-buddhas, who appear wise, kind and peaceful, think about sexual greed and assault in mind. The real purpose behind love for all is loving all women in the world; after enticing the female into the altar for secret empowerment, the guru will have sex with the disciples. The lamas endeavor to practice diligently, only with the lower half of their bodies. This is the Tantric practice of sexual misconduct, which is not allowed in the Buddhist precepts.

The living-buddha, who is actually a political lama, comes to pray for blessings under the guise of religion; we should be very careful that it is a disaster but not a blessing. Speaking of the elimination of disaster and bad fortune, and mumbling mantras, they look like praying for blessings but with sexual desire in mind, and with the show of political and monetary purposes as well. They absorb all resources that they can get with the announced excuse of eliminating disaster for victims, but gather money and play with beautiful females in secret. The contents of Lamaism are only drinking alcohol, eating meat and playing with women. They can never deny the real face of the Couple-Practice Tantra.

The copulation, alcohol, meat, scandal and sexual slave are the contents of the *tantirc* dharma assembly; during the couple-practice, the red and the white *bodhis* are generated; they are actually the obscene fluids from the copulation. The so-called bright-drop and the nectar pill are in fact feces, urine and obscene fluids.

The skull and the drum of human skin are dirty dharma instruments. With the eyes of perverts to look at females, the lamas think about the union of *vajra* and lotus; when they look at females like that way, they want to copulate with them for couple practice; when the lamas, who always think about money and sex, look at your wife, they are thinking

> 若視女人色眯眯，意圖雙身性交戲；
> 唯見財色之喇嘛，瞪著你妻亦色眯。
> 若被設計當佛母，畢竟以淫爲其身；
> 若與喇嘛搞雙修，共譜邪淫諸樂章。

　　說穿了，喇嘛們就是向學佛人注射邪淫毒針的淫蟲。再三爆發性侵事件以及說謊遮掩的喇嘛教，也是使了知內情的人們覺得顫慄的宗教；因爲眾生無知，往往被他們高超而且同聲一氣的說謊技術所矇騙，修學久了以後，女人就被喇嘛們假藉佛法實證的謊言性侵成功，而且自願成爲喇嘛們永遠的情人，幫助喇嘛們圓謊。苦的是家裡不知情的丈夫們，可就綠帽罩頂而不自知了。咱們台灣男人難道就不能覺醒嗎？還要坐視自己頭上的綠帽繼續存在嗎？吾人實在於心不忍，於是頌曰：

> 紅袍綠帽等吟唱，生殖崇拜之底細，
> 原始野蠻性崇拜，人骨法器邪靈降，
> 高價加持騙無知。確保您底血汗錢，
> 亦護妻女之安全，拒當沉默的羔羊。
> 千金難買早知道，後悔沒有特效藥；
> 還請認清眞面目，遠離喇嘛護家眷。
> 邪教之惡招天災，公布密宗綠帽廠；
> 此名藏傳之佛教，喇嘛活佛遍地有；
> 皆是喇嘛教淫蟲，假冒佛教之令名；
> 實非佛教假名稱，李代桃僵壞佛教。
> 混淆宗教與是非，藏傳佛教喇嘛教；
> 乃是山寨版佛教，剽竊佛教名義深；
> 佯裝佛教修行人，私下破戒修雙身，
> 身披袈裟成色狼，欽財騙色是喇嘛。

the same thing.

If the female has become the buddha-mother, she will have sex with the lama finally; if one cultivates couple-practice with the lama, she just pursues the obscene happiness of sexual misconduct.

In fact, the lamas are the satyrs who inject the obscene poison into Buddhist learners' bodies. The lamas have caused many sexual assaults and lie again and again, and their religion makes those who know the truth tremble; due to the ignorance, people are deceived by their consistent, skillful lies, and after practicing for quite a long time, the females are sexually assaulted by the lamas under the lie of Buddhist realization, become the lamas' lovers forever, and help the lamas to tell the lies; but the victims are the husbands who are cuckolded and do not know the truth at all. Can't the Taiwanese men become awakened to it? How can we just stand aside and do nothing about the facts of being cuckolded continuously? We cannot bear to see this and thus make the following verses:

With red robes and green hats, the practice is in fact the worship of reproduction and belongs to the primitive, wild sexual cult; with the dharma instrument of human bone, the evil souls come down; with the expensive prayer, they deceive the ignorant. In order to protect your hard earned money, and your wife and daughters as well, you should step forward and speak aloud. Money cannot buy your regrets, and it is no use crying over spilt milk. Everyone should clearly understand the true face of Lamaism and keep far away from the lamas in order to protect the family. The evil religion causes the disaster, and the secret of Tibetan Buddhism should be disclosed. The so-called Tibetan Buddhism, with lamas and living-buddhas everywhere, is actually the obscene satyrs of Lamaism under the guise of Buddhism. Stealing the name of Buddhism, they replace the good with the evil and destroy Buddhism. Tibetan Buddhism, or called Lamaism, confuses people about the religion and right or wrong; they are in fact the fake Buddhism which steals the terms from Buddhism; they disguise themselves as Buddhist practitioners, but cultivate the Couple-Practice Tantra in secret and break the precepts; the lamas are the satyrs in Buddhist robes, and they deceive people for both money and sex. The Tantric practitioners cheat the female for sex; the living-buddhas in red robes make their sex dreams; they practice it in the secret altar at night; the female practitioner becomes a prostitute, and

竊玉偷香之徒眾，紅袍活佛做春夢；
暗夜密壇魅影幢，密宗女性成公車，
修密喇嘛皆可上；家中丈夫都不知，
自己頭上綠帽堅。

密宗淫亂烏金土，輪轉三塗不能出；
世尊清淨明誨誡，楞嚴經中早預記；
博愛口號正響時，喇嘛紅禍正入侵。

神聖包裝之密宗，千年祕笈大公開：
密宗神秘之面紗，廣行大樂忍不洩。
所有女性勿盲崇，一切丈夫要小心；
遠離密宗喇嘛教，否則盡皆被狼吻。
西藏喇嘛大騙局，正統佛教千年殤。
蒙古當年血淚史，信受喇嘛教雙修，
亂交梅毒大氾濫，種族幾乎將滅絕。

密宗喇嘛愛亂搞，假佛一騙已千年；
淫人妻女笑呵呵，酒色財氣樣樣精；
心中覬覦您配偶，謊稱雙修非行淫；
實修性交名止觀，謊稱成佛必經路；
實則千年大謊言，癡人盡禍甚天災。

性交修行能成佛？喇嘛愚信之迷思。
同入地獄之伴侶，無知毀滅的開始。
密宗道場處處有，喇嘛獵女無時無。

淫人妻女喇嘛教，世紀騙局現形記；
揭開達賴喇嘛群，不爲人知之面目。
千年世紀大淫賊，邪淫喇嘛非佛教；

all lamas can have sex with her; her husband does not know the truth at all and still wear a green hat firmly.

The obscene Tantric practice will lead to the rebirth in the land of Orgyen and let people transmigrate in the three evil paths endlessly; the World-Honored One had taught and warned it clearly; as predicted in the *Surangama Sutra,* when the slogan of "love for all" is promoted, it comes the time of the red disasters by the lamas.

The millennial secret about Tibetan Buddhism in disguise is disclosed now: The true face of Tantric practice behind the veil is having sex and enjoying the bliss without ejaculation. All females should not follow the practice blindly, and all husbands should be careful; they should keep themselves far away from Tibetan Buddhism to avoid being harmed by the satyrs of Lamaism. The Tibetan Lamaism is a great fraud; the orthodox Buddhism has been damaged for a millennium. As the painful experience in Mongolian history, people believed in Lamaism and cultivated the Couple-Practice Tantra; as a result, syphilis (a sexually transmitted disease) spread in the whole country, and the race was almost extinct.

The Tantric lamas love to sleep around, and the fake buddhas have cheated people for a millennium; they enjoy having sex with others' wives and daughters, and are good at alcohol, sex and money fraud; they intend to have sex with your wife, but lie that the couple-practice is not copulation; they call the actual practice of copulation as tranquility and insight, and lie that this is the way must be practiced for Buddhahood; it is really a great millennial lie; the disaster created by these fools is even more severe than the natural disaster.

Can one become a Buddha through the practice of copulation? It is a myth from the blind belief of the lamas. This is the start of ignorance and destruction, and one will go with the lamas to the hell finally. There are Tantric cultivation centers everywhere; the lamas hunt for the girls all the time.

The practice of Lamaism is to have sex with others' wives and daughters; it is a millennial fraud; now we disclose the secret of the Dalai Lama and his followers, which is known by very few people. They are the satyrs in the last millennium; the obscene Lamaism is not Buddhism; basically,

> 本是諸魔假佛名，爲貪精氣而僞傳。
> 僞佛邪法假和尚，雙身修法加性侵。
> 政治伴奏譜淫曲，性侵加上廣斂財。
> 誑騙社會之大眾，嚴重混淆您視聽；
> 進而誤導學佛人，步入曠劫不復境。
>
> 今幸正覺菩薩眾，出世破邪暨顯正；
> 住持正法護法行，高舉破邪大法幢。
> 千年降魔看今朝，戮力降魔護眾生；
> 還我佛教清淨行，顯示喇嘛邪淫性；
> 真相覺醒今歸途，但使正覺菩薩在，
> 不教喇嘛亂人間！

　　爲了教化世人了知密宗喇嘛教的真實本質，於是正覺同修會、正覺教育基金會的所有菩薩們，在達賴喇嘛假藉八八風災來台造勢及斂財時，揭竿而起，在台灣高雄展開了教化社會人士以及導正佛教徒的菩薩行，將近四百人正式展開了陣容浩大的宣示：「**修雙身法的喇嘛教不是佛教。**」才會有這一本宣化紀實的書本編輯及印製出來，繼續教化社會人士，別再讓喇嘛們把山精鬼魅化現的假佛、假菩薩招引來台，以免未來招惹出更大的天災。紀念這次社會教化之大行，於是頌曰：

> 正法菩薩慈悲行，慈悲獅吼護法行；
> 摧破邪淫喇嘛教，遍地紅火邪見滅。
> 澆熄喇嘛之魅火，千年妖魅現形記；
> 救護眾生免災殃，正覺菩薩獅子吼。
> 振聲發聵警魔眾，捍衛佛陀之正法，
> 回歸如來之本懷。

they are the demos disguised as Buddhas and give false teachings because of their greed for the virility. The Tantric practice is a combination of the false buddha, evil dharma, fake monk, Couple-Practice Tantra and sexual assault. They cultivate sexual practice, perform political activity, commit sexual assault and accumulate money. They lie to the public, confuse your insight and even mislead the learners into the bad situation never to be recovered.

Fortunately, now the bodhisattvas of the True Enlightenment step forward to refute the evil teachings and speak the true dharma; they propagate and protect the true dharma, and raise the gonfalon of destroying the false. The millennial demons will be conquered now; to protect people, we must endeavor to ruin the demons; through revealing the obscene nature of Lamaism, we can make Buddhism clean and pure again; through the realization of the truth, one can return to the right way; if the bodhisattvas of the True Enlightenment are here, they will prohibit the lamas from disturbing people.

In order to educate people on the real essence of Tantric Lamaism, many bodhisattvas of both True Enlightenment Practitioners Association and True Enlightenment Education Foundation step forward and perform, in Kaohsiung, the activity of educating people and correcting the behavior of Buddhists during the visit of the Dalai Lama, whose purposes are for drum-up support and money; near four hundreds persons formally proclaim: *"Lamaism, with the Couple-Practice Tantra, is not Buddhism!"* This is the cause of publishing this book, which records the details of the event, so that we can continue educating people; therefore, the lamas will not be able to invite the ghosts and spirits, who disguised themselves as the Buddhas and bodhisattvas, to enter Taiwan, and we can avoid a bigger disaster in the future. The following verses record the great activity of this social education:

The bodhisattvas of the True Enlightenment perform a compassionate conduct and make a compassionate lion roar to protect the dharma; they destroy the obscene Lamaism and extinguish the red fire and evil views everywhere. The ghost fire of Lamaism has been extinguished, and the millennial demon is forced to manifest in its original form; in order to protect sentient beings, the bodhisattvas of the True Enlightenment make the lion roar. They make the loud sound to warn those demons and fight for the Buddha's true dharma so that the Buddhist doctrine can

正覺獅吼震十方，豈容群魔續猖狂；
破邪顯正港都行，一舉撼動佛教界。
揭發喇嘛教眞相，破盡千年之謊言；
菩薩驅魔首部曲，金獅怒吼挽狂瀾；
廣續揭露邪教毒，香巴拉狼之輓歌；
依智斷迷斥喇嘛，不許千年騙局存。
無所不黑之面紗，破解密宗之迷咒；
認清糖衣內毒藥，亦破無效之祈福。
捍衛佛法擊鼓行，拔除佛教獅身蟲；
揭開密宗假面目，阻斷邁向地獄程。
藏傳佛教應正名：無上瑜伽喇嘛教；
密歸密兮佛歸佛，魚目不可混明珠。
信受喇嘛教之人，最終宿命定雙修；
若要免除綠帽蓋，先阻女眷學密宗。
認清喇嘛非佛教：達賴爲首喇嘛輩，
只是一群好色徒，誘你美妻搞性交，
還要您的辛苦錢。家中有人學密者，
小心人財兩皆失；若是哪天東窗爆，
再要回首已難堪。

正覺菩薩護正法，和平理性提訴求：
喇嘛不是佛教徒，請還給佛教清淨。
眞相無畏的力量，於群魔飛舞時代；
菩薩護法團結力，正使達賴淫夢破。
千年騙局今揭露，不讓百姓再遭殃；
認清美麗底謊言，解脫情執之束縛。
末路魔教代言人，今遭正法菩薩破。

return to its original meanings.

The lion roar of the True Enlightenment shakes all worlds in ten directions and does not allow the demons continue to behave savagely; in order to refute the evil and spread the truth, they went to Kaohsiung; this activity shakes the Buddhist society. They expose the truth of Lamaism and refute the millennial Tantric lies; this is the first action of the bodhisattvas to expel the demons; the golden lions roar angrily to remedy the bad situation; they continue to disclose the poison of the evil religion; this is the dirge of Sambhala's satyrs; we should eliminate our confusion according to wisdom and denounce the lamas; the millennial fraud should not exist any more. The black veil is everywhere, and the confusing Tantric mantra should be decoded; the bodhisattvas let people clearly understand the poison coating with sugar and refute the useless prayer. They guard the Buddha dharma with the drum hitting and take the insects in the Buddhist lion away; uncovering the mask of Tibetan Buddhism, they keep people away from the path of hell. The name of Tibetan Buddhism should be corrected as: the Lamaism of the Highest Yoga Tantra. The Tantric practice belongs to Tantrism and the Buddhist practice belongs to Buddhism; they should not be confused. Those who believe in Lamaism are doomed to cultivate the Couple-Practice Tantra. If one wants to avoid being cuckolded, he should prevent his female family members from learning the Tantric practice. We should understand that Lamaism is not Buddhism; the Dalai Lama and his followers are the satyrs; they seduce your beautiful wife for copulation and want to have your hard earned money as well. Those who have family members leaning the Tantric practice should be careful not to lose both family members and money; once the sexual scandal breaks, it will be too late to regret.

The bodhisattvas of the True Enlightenment guard the true dharma and peacefully claim: Lamaism is not Buddhism, and we will make Buddhism clean and pure again. The power of truth and fearlessness appears at the age of many demons existing; the cooperating power of bodhisattvas' dharma protection makes the Dalai Lama's obscene dream broken. The millennial fraud is disclosed now, and people will no longer become the victims; everyone should clearly understand the beautiful lie and be

> 請保護您底女眷，終結喇嘛教謊言；
>
> 務必對喇嘛說不，拒當活佛之性奴。
>
> 斂財性侵謊言破，今成喇嘛之噩夢。

　　最後，我們要向達賴喇嘛提出一個根本問題：佛教許多經典中都說「佛佛道同」，也就是不論哪一尊佛所說的佛法之道，都是與其他諸佛所說完全一樣；所以必須與一切諸佛所說的成佛之道完全相同的，才是真正的佛法。然而，達賴所率領的喇嘛教自創的密宗佛，竟然是將 釋迦牟尼佛所破斥的淫欲貪樂境界，取來作為成佛之道，這與十方諸佛所說的成佛之道全然相違背，正是「佛佛道不同」，不是「佛佛道同」，這樣的雙身法追求遍身樂受的喇嘛邪淫法，還能說是佛法嗎？

這是藏傳「佛教」雙身法的「佛像」，密宗喇嘛與您的妻子就暗中這樣合修無上瑜伽、大樂光明；他們有時也以坐姿進行，猶如上圖所顯示，您就這樣被喇嘛們暗中戴上了綠帽子。

liberated from the fetters of passionate attachment. The spokesman of the ending evil religion is refuted by the bodhisattvas of the true dharma. Please protect your female family members and terminate the lie of Lamaism; you should say no to the lamas and refuse to become the sexual slave of living-buddha. The lies of getting money and sexual assault have been denounced, and now it becomes the nightmare of lamas.

Lastly, we would like to ask the Dalai Lama a fundamental question: Many Buddhist sutras state that "every Buddha gives the same teachings;" it means the teachings of any Buddha, whoever He is, should be exactly the same as all other Buddhas; hence the true Buddha dharma for Buddhahood must be exactly the same as that of all Buddhas. However, Lamaism, led by the Dalai Lama, takes the happiness state of obscene desire, which had been refuted by the Buddha, as the way to Buddhahood. It completely conflicts with the way to Buddhahood taught by all Buddhas in ten directions, and is exactly the case of "not every Buddha gives the same teachings," rather than "every Buddha gives the same teachings." Can such a Couple-Practice Tantra, which is the obscene practice of Lamaism pursuing the whole-body bliss, be called the Buddha dharma?

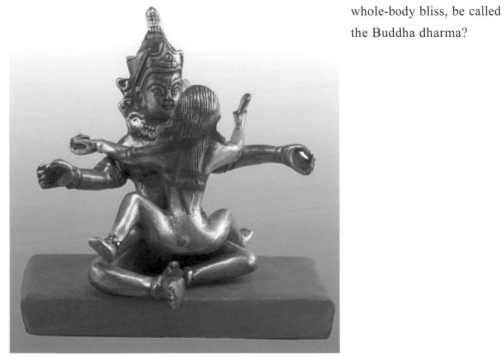

This is the couple-body "buddha statue" of Tibetan "Buddhism." The Tantric lama is privately doing the couple-practice of the Highest Yoga Tantra (radiance of bliss) with your wife like this; sometimes, they do the couple-practice in a sitting posture, just like the photograph shown above; in such a way, you are the man wearing a green hat given secretly by the

The totem of sex and reproduction worship (the sexual organs of both sexes), publicly standing in front of a Tantric temple of Tibetan "Buddhism," shows that Tibetan Buddhism always preaches the Couple-Practice Tantra, which comes from the Hinduism and pursues the obscene happiness of copulation. The pictures are retrieved from the website: http://www.xzta.gov.cn/rwxz/zjw

西藏密宗藏傳「佛教」寺院門口公開展示的生殖崇拜圖騰——男女性器官,顯示密宗所弘揚的從來都是取自印度教的男女性交追求淫樂的雙身法。圖片引用自:
http://www.xzta.gov.cn/rwxz/zjw

附錄三、達賴雙身法舉證

　　如本書第 61 頁所舉，達賴在《達賴：心與夢的解析》中提到，修雙身法者要用吸管練習吸取牛奶，此部分 平實導師在《狂密與眞密》書中早就公開破斥達賴喇嘛等密宗喇嘛教的說法，因此達賴所說射出後吸回原處仍是邪說。列舉如下：

　　【復次，密宗常以上師是否能於合修雙身法時，達到大樂而享受射精之至樂後，復將射出之精液吸回腹中而上提遍於全身，作爲上師是否眞已具足傳授密法之證量。然此邪見有大過失：謂射精後，重新吸回身中時，已非吸回精囊中，而是吸回膀胱，與尿液混雜，稍後仍將因爲尿急而排出體外，有何「不損精氣」之可言者？若謂「吸回膀胱中，無礙於提取精液之淨分」者，其言與實情不符，精液已與尿液混雜故；除非能另行發明一法，將尿液與精液之氣分隔離。是故密宗所主張：「不能射精後重新吸回腹中者，不可修證雙身法」之明禁，以及主張：「若有重新吸回腹中之功夫者，即可與一切女人合修雙身法，包括比丘尼、母、女、姨母、舅母等皆可合修」之明禁行，如是等三昧耶十四根本戒，其實皆是依於外道邪見而施設之戒禁取見也。

　　復次，享受大樂而射精後，吸取淨分者，何如令其留存身中繼續安住而不令出？不如世俗氣功之直接上提，更加有益自身也，何須行淫令出而後吸之？多此一舉也。復次，密宗所修由異性身中吸取淫液淨分之行，同於中國房中術採陰補陽之妄想，縱使眞能採陰補陽，裨益自己色身，又何益於佛法之修證乎！其實與佛法解脫道及佛菩提道悉皆

Appendix C Evidence of the Dalai Lama's involvement in Couple-Practice Tantra

As cited in this book, page 62, the Dalai Lama states, in a book by Francisco J. Varela, *Sleeping, Dreaming and Dying,* that the practitioners of Couple-Practice Tantra need to practice how to draw milk back using a straw. Such a statement from the Dalai Lama, or Tantric Lamaism, has been publicly refuted by Venerable Pings Xiao in his book *The Wanton versus True Secret Schools* (English version entitled *The Façade behind Tibetan Buddhism*). Hence, the Dalai Lama's claim about drawing the ejaculated semen back to its original place is still an evil teaching. The refutations are as follows:

Furthermore, Tibetan Buddhism usually uses the criterion that if a guru can, after enjoying the bliss of ejaculation, draw his ejaculated semen back into the abdomen and spread it to the whole body to qualify if he has the level of achievement to teach the Tantric practice. However, this evil view has the following mistake: When the ejaculated semen is drawn back, it will enter the bladder and mix with urine rather than enter the seminal vesicles; finally it will be drained out of the body together with urine; how could it be claimed as "not loosing the seminal Chi?" The claim about "drawing back into the bladder without interfering with the purification of semen" is not consistent with the fact because the semen has mixed with urine already, unless one can invent another method to separate the seminal Chi from urine. Therefore, the prohibitions of "Those who cannot draw the ejaculated semen back into the abdomen should not cultivate the Couple-Practice Tantra," "Those who can draw the ejaculated semen back into the abdomen can co-practice the Couple-Practice Tantra with any woman, including the nun, his mother, his daughter, his aunts, etc.," and so on, which Tibetan Buddhism claims as the fourteen root precepts of Samaya, are in fact all the wrong prohibitions set up according to the non-Buddhist evil views.

After enjoying the bliss and ejaculating, how can one keep the ejaculated semen inside the body and absorb its purified part? It is inferior to the worldly Chi-practice which can directly make the Chi ascend and benefit the body, without the need to ejaculate the semen out and then draw it back; it is a redundant work. Another method of Tibetan Buddhism is to absorb the purified part of obscene liquid from the opposite sex partner, which is the same as the delusion of absorbing the energy from the female to enrich the male in Chinese sexual technique; even if it is true and can benefit the body, it cannot benefit the practice of the Buddha

無干也。以如是外道法修證、與佛法無關之密宗上師，而遵崇之遠過於佛，豈非顛倒想耶？密教既然不肯依釋尊所說之法爲主爲歸，而依密教上師等人爲主爲歸，而諸密宗上師所弘之法復又全是外道法，悉與解脫道及佛菩提道完全無關，則可了知密教絕非佛教；何以故？謂彼等所說諸法，悉皆不能與佛說諸經互相比對印證故，悉皆與佛說諸經法義互相違背故，由是可知密教絕非佛教也。】（《狂密與眞密》第四輯，頁 1330-1332。）

【復次，密宗以觀想明點，及寶瓶氣修鍊，而能於射精後，將明妃下體中之自身所射精液及明妃淫液吸回腹中之功夫，作爲修學雙身法而證「佛地」功德之資糧者，其實荒謬無知；所以者何？謂彼等縱能修鍊成就此功夫者，亦仍與修證佛法之資糧無關也，唯與密宗自設之雙身法修學資格有關故。

平實今於此書中將密宗最大之秘密公開，令天下人從此皆知其謬：「密宗自設此法，作爲能否修學雙身法之資格限制者，其實完全無義；此謂密宗法王、喇嘛、上師，縱能於射精後再從明妃（或名空行母、佛母）下體中，將明妃之淫液及自己之精液吸回自己腹中，言能增益自己色身者，實乃不明事相之言，亦是自欺欺人之言，何以故？謂吸回後，實際上仍未能保住吸回身中之自己精液，亦未能保住吸入身中之明妃淫液；此因密宗諸師於吸回腹中時，並非吸回精囊中故，只是吸回膀胱，與尿液混合在一處而已；稍後仍將隨同尿液排出體外，是故此功夫從禪益自己色身

dharma at all and in fact has completely nothing to do with the practice of the Liberation-Way and the Buddhahood-Way of the Buddha dharma. However, those Tantric gurus, who practice the non-Buddhist methods that are irrelevant to the Buddha dharma, are promoted and respected far beyond the Buddha; isn't it really ridiculous? Tibetan Buddhism does not follow the teachings of The World-Honored One but follows the Tantric gurus, whose teachings are all non-Buddhist methods and have completely nothing to do with the Liberation-Way and the Buddhahood-Way. Consequently, we can know Tibetan Buddhism is by no means Buddhism since its teachings all conflict with the doctrines of the Buddha's sutras and cannot be contrasted with or proven by the sutras. It is not Buddhism at all. (*The Wanton versus True Secret Schools,* Vol. 4, p.1330-1332, English version entitled *The Façade behind Tibetan Buddhism*)

In addition, Tibetan Buddhism uses the capability of drawing one's ejaculated semen and the female consort's obscene liquid, through the practice of visualizing the bright-drop and Vase-Chi, from the consort's lower body back to his abdomen as the criterion of actually realizing the "Buddha ground" through the Couple-Practice Tantra; it is in fact ridiculous and ignorant. Why? Even if they can attain this capability, it is irrelevant to the realization of the Buddha dharma, but only relates to the qualification of practicing the Couple-Practice Tantra, which is set by Tibetan Buddhism itself.

In this book, Pings will disclose the most confidential secret and let the public all know its fallacy:

Tibetan Buddhism sets this method as the qualification if one can practice the Couple-Practice Tantra or not; it is in fact completely nonsense. Even the Tantric dharma-king, lama or guru can draw his ejaculated semen and the female consort's (or called *dakini* or buddha-mother) obscene liquid from the consorts' private parts back to his abdomen and claims it can benefit his physical body, he is in fact ignorant of the truth and cheats himself and others. Why? The truth is that the ejaculated semen and the consort's obscene liquid are drawn back into his bladder and mix with urine, rather than into his seminal vesicles; later on, the ejaculated semen and the consort's obscene liquid will be drained out from his body together with urine; he cannot keep them in the body finally. Therefore, from the point of benefiting one's body, this practice is actually useless, not to mention helping the practice and realization of the Buddhahood-Way. (*The Wanton*

而觀之，實無作用可言也，何況能助益佛道之修證？」】（《狂
密與眞密》第四輯，頁 1357-1358。）

（其他藏傳佛教喇嘛教更詳細雙身法的邪說，

　請參閱《狂密與眞密》共四輯的舉證。）

　　因此，由 平實導師已在《狂密與眞密》中做了詳盡的舉證，大
家就可以知道「藏傳佛教」雙身法的底細。假設達賴或諸喇嘛們，
看到了這些文字，還欲狡辯而稱說：「有人說：『修密宗雙身法將
明點（精液）射出後是吸回膀胱。』那是不對的說法，因爲我們
藏傳佛教乃是將射出的明點（精液）吸回原處（頭頂或精囊）。」
若達賴爲首的喇嘛們有此類辯解之說法，不僅是無稽之談，根本就
是爲了圓謊而繼續說謊。不論於佛法正理或現代醫學生理上的說
明，都知道他們這種說法乃是錯謬的；因爲藏傳佛教達賴喇嘛所說
的明點是指精液，又說明點原來的處所是在頭部而非精囊，其意即
是精液儲放的處所是在頭部，乃是自相矛盾的說法，純屬狡辯之詞，
只有迷信之人才會信受。只有當大家都更瞭解達賴這個黔驢技窮農
奴主的騙術後，不再被喇嘛教假借「藏傳佛教」的名義來籠罩，而
能更理智地瞭解眞正的三乘佛教與修學雙身法的喇嘛教之間的差
異，才能讓佛法久住長存，利樂人天。

versus True Secret Schools, Vol. 4, p. 1357-1358, English version entitled *The Façade behind Tibetan Buddhism*)

For more details about the evil teachings of the Couple-Practice Tantra of Tibetan Buddhism, or Lamaism, please refer to the evidence provided in *The Wanton versus True Secret Schools,* four volumes in total.
(English version entitled *The Façade behind Tibetan Buddhism*)

Thus, from the detailed evidence in *The Wanton versus True Secret Schools* by Venerable Pings, everyone can clearly know about all the exact details of Couple-Practice Tantra of "Tibetan Buddhism." If the Dalai Lama, or any lama, sees this statement, they might try to argue with sophistry: "Someone says, '**In cultivating the Couple-Practice Tantra of Tibetan Tantric School, the practitioners draw the ejaculated bright-drop** (semen) **back into the bladder.**' The above saying is incorrect. For us, the practitioners of Tibetan Buddhism draw the ejaculated bright-drop (semen) back to its original place (the crown of the head or the seminal vesicles)." If the lamas, led by the Dalai Lama, defend their view with such a statement, their argument is not only groundless, but also only to justify themselves to continue their lies. From the perspective of either correct Buddhist doctrines or modern medical physiology, their argument is totally wrong. According to the Dalai Lam of Tibetan Buddhism, the so-called bright-drop refers to the semen and the original place of the bright-drop is in the head rather than the seminal vesicles. What he means is precisely that the semen is stored in the head. The Dalai Lama's argument is not only self-contradictory but also purely specious; only those who are superstitious will believe his words. Only when everyone has a better understanding of the deceitful tricks by the Dalai Lama, who is a lord of serfs at his wit's end, will not be deceived by Lamaism under the guise of "Tibetan Buddhism," and can tell the differences between the true three-vehicle Buddhism and Lamaism (which cultivates the Couple-Practice Tanta) in a more rational way, we can make the Buddhism live longer to benefit the human and celestial beings.

上圖是密宗喇嘛教雙身「佛像」，是男女雙修的性交圖；若那個與喇嘛性交女性是您的家人，您將情何以堪？

The above picture is the couple-body "buddha statue" of Tantric Lamaism, a picture of the couple-practice of copulation. If the woman copulating with a lama is your family member, how can you endure this?

佛教正覺同修會各地共修處：

台北正覺講堂：

台北市承德路三段二七七號九樓（捷運淡水線圓山站旁）

電話：(02)2595-7295（請於晚上共修時聯繫）

(分機號碼：九樓 10、11。十樓 15、16。五樓 18、19。十樓書局 14。)

大溪正覺祖師堂：

桃園縣大溪鎮美華里信義路六五〇巷坑底五之六號

電話：(03)388-6110

桃園正覺講堂：

桃園市介壽路二八六、二八八號十樓（陽明運動公園對面）

電話：(03)374-9363（請於週六早上、或晚上共修時聯繫）

新竹正覺講堂：

新竹市南大路二四一號三樓（竹蓮市場附近）

電話：(03)561-9020（請於晚上共修時聯繫）

台中正覺講堂：

台中市南屯區五權西路二段六六六號十三樓之四（國泰世華銀十三樓）

電話：(04)2381-6090（請於晚上共修時聯繫）

台南正覺講堂：

台南市西門路四段十五號四樓（民德國中北側京城銀行四樓）

電話：(06)282-0541（請於晚上共修時聯繫）

高雄正覺講堂：

高雄市中正三路四十五號五樓（復興中正路口捷運信義國小站旁）

電話：(07)223-4248（請於晚上共修時聯繫）

美國洛杉磯正覺講堂：

17979 E. Arenth Ave, Unit B, City of Industry, CA 91748 USA

Tel. (626) 965-2200　　Cell. (626) 454-0607

正覺同修會網址：http://www.a202.idv.tw

正覺同修會所有結緣書內容之閱讀或下載：

成佛之道網站：http://www.a202.idv.tw

正智出版社　書香園地：http://books.enlighten.org.tw

The Cultivation Centers
of the True Enlightenment Practitioners Association

Taipei True Enlightenment Lecture Hall:
9th Fl., No. 277, Sec. 3, Chengde Rd., Taipei, Taiwan, R.O.C.
Tel. (at night): (02)2595-7295
(Extension: 10 & 11 for 9th fl., 15 & 16 for 10th fl., 18 & 19 for 5th fl., and 14 for the bookstore on 10th fl.)

Daxi True Enlightenment Patriarch Hall
No.5-6, Kengdi, Ln. 650, Xinyi Rd., Daxi Township, Taoyuan County 335, Taiwan, R.O.C.
Tel.: (03)388-6110

Taoyuan True Enlightenment Lecture Hall:
10th Fl., No. 286 & 288, Jieshou Rd., Taoyuan, Taiwan, R.O.C.
Tel. (Saturday morning): (03)374-9363

Hsinchu True Enlightenment Lecture Hall:
3rd Fl., No. 241, Nanda Rd., Hsinchu, Taiwan, R.O.C.
Tel. (at night): (03)561-9020

Taichung True Enlightenment Lecture Hall:
13 Fl.-4, No. 666, Sec. 2, Wuquan W. Rd., Nantun Dist., Taichung, Taiwan, R.O.C.
Tel. (at night): (04)2381-6090

Tainan True Enlightenment Lecture Hall:
4th Fl., No. 15, Sec. 4, Ximen Rd., Tainan, Taiwan, R.O.C.
Tel. (at night): (06)282-0541

Kaohsiung True Enlightenment Lecture Hall:
5th Fl., No. 45, Zhongzheng 3rd Rd., Kaohsiung, Taiwan, R.O.C.
Tel. (at night): (07)223-4248

Los Angeles True Enlightenment Lecture Hall
17979 E. Arenth Ave, Unit B, City of Industry, CA 91748 USA
Tel.:(626) 965-2200   Cell.:(626) 454-0607

Website of the True Enlightenment Practitioners Association:
http://www.a202.idv.tw

Download for all free publications of the True Enlightenment

Practitioners Association, Website of the Way to Buddhahood:
http://www.a202.idv.tw

Website of the True Wisdom Publishing Co.:
http://books.enlighten.org.tw

正智出版社有限公司書籍介紹

宗門正眼──公案拈提第一輯

【作者】平實導師
【出版日期】1997年7月【書號】957-28743-3-0
【開本】菊16開，546頁【定價】新台幣 500元

繼承克勤圓悟大師碧巖錄宗旨之禪門鉅作。先則舉示當代大法師之邪說，消弭當代禪門大師鄉愿之心態，摧破當今禪門「世俗禪」之妄談；次則旁通教法，表顯宗門正理；繼以道之次第，消弭古今狂禪；後藉言語及文字機鋒，直示宗門入處。悲智雙運，禪味十足，數百年來難得一睹之禪門鉅著也。（原初版書《禪門摩尼寶聚》，改版後補充為五百餘頁新書，總計多達二十四萬字，內容更精彩，並改名為《宗門正眼》，讀者原購初版《禪門摩尼寶聚》皆可寄回本公司免費換新，免附回郵，亦無截止期限）

禪淨圓融

【作者】平實導師
【出版日期】1997年7月【書號】957-98597-8-7
【開本】菊16開，214頁【定價】新台幣 200元

言淨土諸祖所未曾言，示諸宗祖師所未曾示；禪淨圓融，另闢成佛捷徑，兼顧自力他力，闡釋淨土門之速行易行道，亦同時揭櫫聖教門之速行易行道；令廣大淨土行者得免緩行難證之苦，亦令聖道門行者得以藉著淨土速行道而加快成佛之時劫。乃前無古人之超勝見地，非一般弘揚禪淨法門典籍也，先讀為快。

真實如來藏

【作者】平實導師
【出版日期】1997年12月【書號】957-98597-5-2
【開本】菊16開，319頁【定價】新台幣 400元

如來藏真實存在，乃宇宙萬有之本體，並非印順法師、達賴喇嘛等人所說之「唯有名相、無此心體」。如來藏是涅槃之本際，是一切有智之人竭盡心智、不斷探索而不能得之生命實相；是古今中外許多大師自以為悟而當面錯過之生命實相。如來藏即是阿賴耶識，乃是一切有情本自具足、不生不滅之真實心。當代中外大師於此書出版之前所未能言者，作者於本書中盡情流露、詳細闡釋。真悟者讀之，必能增益悟境、智慧增上；錯悟者讀之，必能檢討自己之錯誤，免犯大妄語業；未悟者讀之，能知參禪之理路，亦能以之檢查一切名師是否真悟。此書是一切哲學家、宗教家、學佛者及欲昇華心智之人必讀之鉅著。

禪─悟前與悟後

【作者】平實導師【出版日期】1997年12月
【書號】957-98597-9-5 / 957-97840-0-0
【開本】菊16開，上下冊【定價】新台幣 500元/套

本書能建立學人悟道之信心與正確知見，圓滿具足而有次第地詳述禪悟之功夫與禪悟之內容，指陳參禪中細微淆訛之處，能使學人明自真心、見自本性。若未能悟入，亦能以正確知見辨別古今中外一切大師究係真悟？或屬錯悟？便有能力揀擇，捨名師而選明師，後時必有悟道之緣。一旦悟道，遲者七次人天往返，便出三界，速者一生取辦。學人欲求開悟者，不可不讀。

宗門法眼─公案拈提第二輯

【作者】平實導師【出版日期】1998年7月
【書號】957-98597-6-0
【開本】菊16開，472頁【定價】新台幣 500元

列舉實例，闡釋土城廣欽老和尚之悟處；並直示這位不識字的老和尚妙智橫生之根由，繼而剖析禪宗歷代大德之開悟公案，解析當代密宗高僧卡盧仁波切之錯悟證據，並例舉當代顯宗高僧、大居士之錯悟證據（凡健在者，為免影響其名聞利養，皆隱其名）。藉辨正當代名師之邪見，向廣大佛子指陳禪悟之正道，彰顯宗門法眼。悲勇兼出，強捋虎鬚；慈智雙運，巧探驪龍；摩尼寶珠在手，直示宗門入處，禪味十足；若非大悟徹底，不能為之。禪門精奇人物，允宜人手一冊，供作參究及悟後印證之圭臬。本書於2008年4月改版，增寫為大約500頁篇幅，以利學人研讀參究時更易悟入宗門正法，以前所購初版首刷及初版二刷舊書，皆可免費換取新書。

楞伽經詳解

【作者】平實導師【出版日期】2003年11月
【書號】957-98597-7-9
【開本】菊16開，共十輯【定價】新台幣 250元/輯

本經是禪宗見道者印證所悟真偽之根本經典，亦是禪宗見道者悟後起修之依據經典；故達摩祖師於印證二祖慧可大師之後，將此經典連同佛缽祖衣一併交付二祖，令其依此經典佛示金言、進入修道位，修學一切種智。由此可知此經對於真悟之人修學佛道，是非常重要之一部經典。此經能破外道邪說，亦破佛門中錯悟名師之謬說，亦破禪宗部分祖師之狂禪：不讀經典、一向主張「一悟即成究竟佛」之謬執。並開示愚夫所行禪、觀察義禪、攀緣如禪、如來禪等差別，令行者對於三乘禪法差異有所分辨；亦糾正禪宗祖師古來對於如來禪之誤解，嗣後可免以訛傳訛之弊。此經亦是法相唯識宗之根本經典，禪者悟後欲修一切種智而入初地者，必須詳讀。

宗門道眼—公案拈提第三輯

【作者】平實導師【出版日期】1999年7月

【書號】957-97840-1-9

【開本】菊16開，354頁【定價】新台幣 500元

繼宗門法眼之後，再以金剛之作略、慈悲之胸懷、犀利之筆觸，舉示寒山、拾得、布袋三大士之悟處，消弭當代錯悟者對於寒山大士……等之誤會及誹謗。 亦舉出民初以來與虛雲和尚齊名之蜀郡鹽亭袁煥仙夫子——南懷瑾老師之師，其「悟處」何在？並蒐羅許多真悟祖師之證悟公案，顯示禪宗歷代祖師之睿智，指陳部分祖師、奧修及當代顯密大師之謬悟，作為殷鑑，幫助禪子建立及修正參禪之方向及知見。假使讀者閱此書已，一時尚未能悟，亦可一面加功用行，一面以此宗門道眼辨別真假善知識，避開錯誤之印證及歧路，可免大妄語業之長劫慘痛果報。欲修禪宗之禪者，務請細讀。

宗門血脈—公案拈提第四輯

【作者】平實導師【出版日期】2000年7月

【書號】957-97840-5-1

【開本】菊16開，主文452頁，全書464頁【定價】新台幣 500元

末法怪象—許多修行人自以為悟，每將無念靈知認作真實；崇尚二乘法諸師及其徒眾，則將外於如來藏之緣起性空—無因論之無常空、斷滅空、一切法空—錯認為 佛所說之般若空性。這兩種現象已於當今海峽兩岸及美加地區顯密大師之中普遍存在；人人自以為悟，心高氣壯，便敢寫書解釋祖師證悟之公案，大多出於意識思惟所得，言不及義，錯誤百出，因此誤導廣大佛子同陷大妄語之地獄業中而不能自知。彼等書中所說之悟處，其實處處違背第一義經典之聖言量。彼等諸人不論是否身披袈裟，都非佛法宗門血脈，或雖有禪宗法脈之傳承，亦只徒具形式；猶如螟蛉，非真血脈，未悟得根本真實故。禪子欲知 佛、祖之真血脈者，請讀此書，便知分曉。

宗通與說通

【作者】平實導師【出版日期】2000年12月

【書號】957-97840-7-8

【開本】菊16開，全書共8章，380頁【定價】新台幣 200元

古今中外，錯誤之人如麻似粟，每以常見外道所說之靈知心，認作真心；或妄想虛空之勝性能量為真如，或錯認物質四大元素藉冥性（靈知心本體）能成就吾人色身及知覺，或認初禪至四禪中之了知心為不生不滅之涅槃心。此等皆非通宗者之見地。復有錯悟之人一向主張「宗門與教門不相干」，此即尚未通達宗門之人也。其實宗門與教門互通不

二，宗門所證者乃是真如與佛性，教門所說者乃說宗門證悟之真如佛性，故教門與宗門不二。本書作者以宗教二門互通之見地，細說「宗通與說通」，從初見道至悟後起修之道、細說分明；並將諸宗諸派在整體佛教中之地位與次第，加以明確之教判，學人讀之即可了知佛法之梗概也。欲擇明師學法之前，允宜先讀。

宗門正道—公案拈提第五輯

【作者】平實導師【出版日期】2001年7月
【書號】957-97840-9-4
【開本】菊16開，主文共496頁，全書512頁【定價】新台幣 500元

修學大乘佛法有二果須證—解脫果及大菩提果。二乘人不證大菩提果，唯證解脫果；此果之智慧，名為聲聞菩提、緣覺菩提。大乘佛子所證二果之菩提果為佛菩提，故名大菩提果，其慧名為一切種智—函蓋二乘解脫果。然此大乘二果修證，須經由禪宗之宗門證悟方能相應。而宗門證悟極難，自古已然；其所以難者，咎在古今佛教界普遍存在三種邪見：1.以修定認作佛法， 2.以無因論之緣起性空—否定涅槃本際如來藏以後之一切法空作為佛法， 3.以常見外道邪見（離語言妄念之靈知性）作為佛法。 如是邪見，或因自身正見未立所致，或因邪師之邪教導所致，或因無始劫來虛妄熏習所致。若不破除此三種邪見，永劫不悟宗門真義、不入大乘正道，唯能外門廣修菩薩行。 平實導師於此書中，有極為詳細之說明，有志佛子欲摧邪見、入於內門修菩薩行者，當閱此書。

狂密與真密

【作者】平實導師【出版日期】2002年2月
【書號】957-30019-1-8
【開本】菊16開，共四輯【定價】新台幣 140元/輯

密教之修學，皆由有相之觀行法門而入，其最終目標仍不離顯教經典所說第一義諦之修證；若離顯教第一義經典、或違背顯教第一義經典，即非佛教。西藏密教之觀行法，如灌頂、觀想、遷識法、寶瓶氣、大聖歡喜雙身修法、喜金剛、無上瑜伽、大樂光明、樂空雙運等，皆是印度教兩性生生不息思想之轉化，自始至終皆以如何能運用交合淫樂之法達到全身受樂為其中心思想，純屬欲界五欲的貪愛，不能令人超出欲界輪迴，更不能令人斷除我見；何況大乘之明心與見性，更無論矣！故密宗之法絕非佛法也。而其明光大手印、大圓滿法教，又皆同以常見外道所說離語言妄念之無念靈知心錯認為佛地之真如，不能直指不生不滅之真如。西藏密宗所有法王與徒眾，都尚未開頂門眼，不能辨別真偽，以依人不依法、依密續不依經典故，不肯將其上師喇嘛所說對照第一義經典，純依密續之藏密祖師所說為準，因此而誇大其證德與證量，動

輒謂彼祖師上師為究竟佛、為地上菩薩；如今台海兩岸亦有自謂其師證量高於 釋迦文佛者，然觀其師所述，猶未見道，仍在觀行即佛階段，尚未到禪宗相似即佛、分證即佛階位，竟敢標榜為究竟佛及地上法王，誑惑初機學人。凡此怪象皆是狂密，不同於真密之修行者。近年狂密盛行，密宗行者被誤導者極眾，動輒自謂已證佛地真如，自視為究竟佛，陷於大妄語業中而不知自省，反謗顯宗真修實證者之證量粗淺；或如義雲高與釋性圓…等人，於報紙上公然誹謗真實證道者為「騙子、無道人、人妖、癩蛤蟆…」等，造下誹謗大乘勝義僧之大惡業；或以外道法中有為有作之甘露、魔術……等法，誑騙初機學人，狂言彼外道法為真佛法。如是怪象，在西藏密宗及附藏密之外道中，不一而足，舉之不盡，學人宜應慎思明辨，以免上當後又犯毀破菩薩戒之重罪。密宗學人若欲遠離邪知邪見者，請閱此書，即能了知密宗之邪謬，從此遠離邪見與邪修，轉入真正之佛道。

宗門正義—公案拈提第六輯

【作者】平實導師【出版日期】2002年8月
【書號】957-30019-6-9
【開本】菊16開，516頁【定價】新台幣 500元

佛教有六大危機，乃是藏密化、世俗化、膚淺化、學術化、宗門密意失傳、悟後進修諸地之次第混淆；其中尤以宗門密意之失傳，為當代佛教最大之危機。由宗門密意失傳故，易令 世尊本懷普被錯解，易令 世尊正法被轉易為外道法，以及加以淺化、世俗化，是故宗門密意之廣泛弘傳與具緣佛弟子，極為重要。然而欲令宗門密意之廣泛弘傳予具緣之佛弟子者，必須同時配合錯誤知見之解析、普令佛弟子知之，然後輔以公案解析之直示入處，方能令具緣之佛弟子悟入。而此二者，皆須以公案拈提之方式為之，方易成其功、竟其業，是故平實導師續作宗門正義一書，以利學人。

心經密意

【作者】平實導師【出版日期】2002年12月
【書號】957-30019-9-3
【開本】平裝 / 314頁 / 25k / 普級【定價】新台幣 300元

本書闡釋心經之密意，亦闡明心經與解脫道之關係，心經與佛菩提道之關係，心經與祖師公案之關係。讀者藉由此書之詳細研讀，配合正確之參禪法門，則易於親證如來藏而進入禪宗明心之開悟境界，亦得因此而進入佛菩提之不可思議智慧境界。

二乘菩提所證之解脫道，實依第八識心之斷除煩惱障現行而立解脫之名；大乘菩提所證之佛菩提道，實依親證第八識如來藏之涅槃性、清淨自性、及其中道性而立般若之名；禪宗祖師公案所證之真心，即是此第八識如來藏；是故三乘佛法所修所證之三乘菩提，皆依此如來藏心而立名也。此第八識心，即是《心經》所說之心也。證得此如來藏已，即能漸入大乘佛菩提道，亦可因證知此心而了知二乘無學所不能知之無餘涅槃本際，是故心經之密意，與三乘佛菩提之關係極為密切、不可分割，三乘佛法皆依此心而立名故。

今者 平實導師以其所證解脫道之無生智、及佛菩提之般若種智，將《心經》與解脫道、佛菩提道、祖師公案之關係與密意，以演講之方式，用淺顯之語句和盤托出，發前人所未言，呈三乘菩提之真義，令人藉此《心經密意》一舉而窺三乘菩提之堂奧，迥異諸方言不及義之說；欲求真實佛智者、不可不讀！

宗門密意—公案拈提第七輯

【作者】平實導師【出版日期】2003年7月
【書號】957-28743-1-4
【開本】菊16開，538頁【定價】新台幣 500元

佛教之世俗化，將導致學人以信仰作為學佛，則將以感應及世間法之庇祐，作為學佛之主要目標，不能了知學佛之主要目標為親證三乘菩提。大乘菩提則以般若實相智慧為主要修習目標，以二乘菩提解脫道為附帶修習之標的；是故學習大乘法者，應以禪宗之證悟為要務，能親入大乘菩提之實相般若智慧中故，般若實相智慧非二乘聖人所能知故。此書則以台灣世俗化佛教之三大法師，說法似是而非之實例，配合真悟祖師之公案解析，提示證悟般若之關節，令學人易得悟入。

淨土聖道—兼評日本本願念佛

【作者】正德老師【出版日期】2003年【書號】957-28743-8-1
【開本】菊16開，全書共5章，279頁【定價】新台幣 200元

佛法甚深極廣，般若玄微，非諸二乘聖僧所能知之，一切凡夫更無論矣！所謂一切證量皆歸淨土是也！是故大乘法中「聖道之淨土、淨土之聖道」，其義甚深，難可了知；乃至真悟之人，初心亦難知也。今有正德老師真實證悟後，復能深探淨土與聖道之緊密關係，憐憫眾生之誤會淨土實義，亦欲利益廣大淨土行人同入聖道，同獲淨土中之聖道門要義，乃振奮心神、書以成文，今得刊行天下。主文279頁，連同序文等共301頁，總有十一萬六千餘字。

起信論講記

【作者】平實導師【出版日期】2005年9月

【書號】957-28743-5-7

【開本】菊16開，共六輯 全部出版完畢【定價】新台幣 200元/ 輯

詳解大乘起信論心生滅門與心真如門之真實意旨，消除以往大師與學人對起信論所說心生滅門之誤解，由是而得了知真心如來藏之非常非斷中道正理；亦因此一講解，令此論以往隱晦而被誤解之真實義，得以如實顯示，令大乘佛菩提道之正理得以顯揚光大；初機學者亦可藉此正論所顯示之法義，對大乘法理生起正信，從此得以真發菩提心，真入大乘法中修學，世世常修菩薩正行。

優婆塞戒經講記

【作者】平實導師【出版日期】2007年9月

【書號】986-81358-2-6

【開本】菊16開 共八輯【定價】新台幣 200元/ 輯

本經詳述在家菩薩修學大乘佛法，應如何受持菩薩戒？對人間善行應如何看待？對三寶應如何護持？應如何正確地修集此世後世證法之福德？應如何修集後世「行菩薩道之資糧」？並詳述第一義諦之正義：五蘊非我非異我、自作自受、異作異受……等深妙法義，乃是修學大乘佛法、行菩薩行之在家菩薩所應當了知者。出家菩薩今世或未來世登地已，捨報之後多數將如華嚴經中諸大菩薩，以在家菩薩身而修行菩薩行，故亦應以此經所述正理而修之，配合《楞伽經、解深密經、楞嚴經、華嚴經》等道次第正理，方得漸次成就佛道；故此經是一切大乘行者皆應證知之正法。

真假活佛—略論附佛外道盧勝彥之邪說

【作者】正犀居士【出版日期】2006年3月

【書號】986-81358-4-2

【開本】菊16開，285頁【定價】新台幣 140元

人人身中都有真活佛，永生不滅而有大神用，但眾生都不了知，所以常被身外的西藏密宗假活佛籠罩欺瞞。本來就真實存在的真活佛，才是真正的密宗無上密！諾那活佛因此而說禪宗是大密宗，但藏密的所有活佛都不知道、也不曾實證自身中的真活佛。本書詳實宣示真活佛的道理，舉證盧勝彥的「佛法」不是真佛法，也顯示盧勝彥是假活佛，直接的闡釋第一義佛法見道的真實正理。真佛宗的所有上師與學人們，都應該詳細閱讀，包括盧勝彥個人在內。

阿含正義—唯識學探源

【作者】平實導師【出版日期】2007年8月
【書號】978-986-81358-6-4 / 986-81358-6-9
【開本】菊16開，共七輯，2464頁【定價】新台幣 250元/ 輯

廣說四大部《阿含經》諸經中隱說之真正義理，一一舉示佛陀本懷，令阿含時期初轉法輪根本經典之真義，如實顯現於佛子眼前。並提示末法大師對於阿含真義誤解之實例，一一比對之，證實唯識增上慧學確於原始佛法之阿含諸經中已隱覆密意而略說之，證實世尊確於原始佛法中已曾密意而說第八識如來藏之總相; 亦證實 世尊在四阿含中已說此藏識是名色十八界之因、之本—證明如來藏是能生萬法之根本心。佛子可據此修正以往受諸大師（譬如西藏密宗應成派中觀師：印順、昭慧、傳道、大願、達賴、宗喀巴、寂天、月稱、…等人）誤導之邪見，建立正見，轉入正道。

超意境CD

【定價】新台幣 280元

以平實導師公案拈提書中超越意境之頌詞，加上曲風優美的旋律，錄成令人嚮往的超意境歌曲，其中包括正覺發願文及平實導師親自譜成的黃梅調歌曲一首。詞曲雋永，殊堪翫味，可供學禪者吟詠，有助於見道。內附設計精美的彩色小冊，解說每一首詞的背景本事。【每購買公案拈提書籍一冊，即贈送一片。】

我的菩提路第一輯

【作者】釋悟圓、釋善藏法師……等人合著
【出版日期】2007年4月【書號】978-986-82992-2-1
【開本】菊16開，335頁【定價】新台幣 200元

凡夫及二乘聖人不能實證的佛菩提證悟，末法時代的今天仍然有人能得實證，由正覺同修會釋悟圓、釋善藏法師等二十餘位實證如來藏者所寫的見道報告，已為當代學人見證宗門正法之絲縷不絕，證明大乘義學的法脈仍然存在，為末法時代求悟般若之學人照耀出光明的坦途。由二十餘位大乘見道者所繕，敘述各種不同的學法、見道因緣與過程，參禪求悟者必讀。

我的菩提路第二輯

【作者】郭正益等著
【出版日期】2010年4月【書號】978-986-6431-07-4
【開本】菊16開，448頁【定價】新台幣 250元

由郭正益老師等人合著，書中詳述彼等諸人歷經各處道場學法，一一修學而加以檢擇之不同過程以後，因閱讀正覺同修會、正智出版社書籍而發起抉擇分，轉入正覺同修會中修學；乃至學法及見道之過程，都一一詳述之。其中張志成等人係由前現代禪轉進正覺同修會，張志成原為現代禪副宗長，以前未閱本會書籍時，曾被人藉其名義著文評論 平實導師（詳見《宗通與說通》辨正及《眼見佛性》書末附錄…等）；後因偶然接觸正覺同修會書籍，深覺以前聽人評論平實導師之語不實，於是投入極多時間閱讀本會書籍、深入思辨，詳細探索中觀與唯識之關聯與異同，認為正覺之法義方是正法，深覺相應；亦解開多年來對佛法的迷雲，確定應依八識論正理修學方是正法。乃不顧面子，毅然前往正覺同修會面見平實導師懺悔，並正式學法求悟。今已與其同修王美伶（亦為前現代禪傳法老師），同樣證悟如來藏而證得法界實相，生起實相般若真智。此書中尚有七年來本會第一位眼見佛性者之見性報告一篇，一同供養大乘佛弟子。

鈍鳥與靈龜——考證後代凡夫對大慧宗杲禪師的無根誹謗

【作者】平實導師【出版日期】2007年11月
【書號】978-986-82992-9-0
【開本】菊16開，全書共14章，435頁【定價】新台幣 250元/ 輯

全書四百餘頁，大乘佛法不論何宗何派傳承，其證悟皆不能外於如來藏妙心；此謂唯一佛乘之證悟祇有一個實相，從無二種或三種實相。禪宗看話禪與默照禪亦不能外於此一真相，此書舉證天童與大慧所悟同屬此心，則古今污蔑大慧禪師之事於今即應終於智者。

維摩詰經講記（1-6輯已全部出版）

【作者】平實導師【出版日期】2008年9月
【書號】978-986-83908-0-5
【開本】菊16開，共6輯，每輯300餘頁【定價】新台幣 200元/ 輯

本經系 世尊在世時，由等覺菩薩維摩詰假藉疾病而演說之大乘菩提無上妙義，所說函蓋甚廣然極簡略，是故今時諸方大師與學人讀之悉皆錯解，何況能知其中隱含之深妙正義，是故普遍無法為人解說；若強為人說，則成依文解義而有諸多過失。今由平實導師公開宣講之後，詳實解釋其中密意，令維摩詰菩薩所說大乘不可思議解脫之深妙正法得以正確宣流於人間，利益當代學人及與諸方大師。書中詳實演述大乘佛法深妙不二智慧境界，顯示諸法之中絕待之實相境界，建立大乘菩

薩妙道於永遠不敗不壞之地，以此成就護法偉功，欲冀永利娑婆人天。
已經宣講圓滿，將整理成書、廣為流通，以利諸方大師及諸學人。

真假外道

【作者】游正光老師【出版日期】2008年6月
【書號】978-986-83908-5-0
【開本】菊16開，224頁【定價】新台幣 200元

本書具體舉證佛門中的常見外道知見實例，並加以教證及理證上的辨
正，幫助讀者輕鬆而快速的了知常見外道的錯誤知見，進而遠離佛門
內外的常見外道知見，因此即能改正修學方向而快速實證佛法。

勝鬘經講記（第1-6輯已全部出版）

【作者】平實導師【出版日期】2009年9月
【書號】978-986-83908-8-1
【開本】菊16開，每輯約350頁
【定價】新台幣 200元/ 輯

勝鬘經所說三乘菩提之異同，於本講記中有深入詳解，顯示菩薩所證
如來藏實相是不共二乘之智慧境界；又兼述二乘所斷一念無明與大乘
所斷無始無明之關聯與含攝，能令學人建立三乘菩提整體知見，兼顧
權實而不再執偏排正、執小謗大，始能真修成佛之道。

如來藏為三乘菩提之所依，若離如來藏心體及其含藏之一切種子，即
無三界有情及一切世間法，亦無二乘菩提緣起性空之出世間法；本經
詳說無始無明、一念無明皆依如來藏而有之正理，藉著詳解煩惱障與
所知障間之關係，令學人深入了知二乘菩提與佛菩提相異之妙理；聞
後即可了知佛菩提之特勝處及三乘修道之方向與原理，邁向攝受正法
而速成佛道的境界中。

楞嚴經講記（第1-10輯已出版）

【作者】平實導師【出版日期】2011年6月
【書號】978-986-6431-04-3
【開本】菊16開【定價】新台幣 200元/ 輯

楞嚴經系密教部之重要經典，亦是顯教中普受重視之經典；經中宣說
明心與見性之內涵極為詳細，將一切法都會歸如來藏，亦闡釋佛菩提
道修學過程中之種種魔境，以及外道誤會涅槃之狀況。然因言句深澀
難解，法義亦復深妙寬廣，學人讀之普難通達，是故讀者大多誤會，不
能如實理解 佛所說之明心與見性內涵，亦因是故多有悟錯之人引為開
悟之證言，成就大妄語罪。今由平實導師詳細講解之後，整理成文，以
易讀易懂之語體文刊行天下，以利學人。

國家圖書館出版品預行編目(CIP)資料

達賴眞面目：玩盡天下女人 / 白志偉等編著. -- 初版.
-- 臺北市：正智，2010.12
面 ；　公分
中英對照
ISBN 978-986-6431-14-2（精裝）

1.藏傳佛教　2.社會倫理

226.96　　　　　　　　　　　　　　100000048

達賴真面目
——玩盡天下女人

編 著 者：白志偉、吳振聲、辛在尊、葉音讚、成種慧、董建昌、吳錫焜
出 版 者：正智出版社有限公司
地　　址：10367 台北市承德路三段 267 號 10 樓
電　　話：886-2-25957295 ext.10-21（請於夜間共修時間聯繫）
傳　　眞：886-2-25954493
國內定價：新臺幣捌佰元
海外定價：美金肆拾伍元
版次日期：初版首刷 2011 年 1 月 1500 冊
版次日期：初版二刷 2011 年 6 月 1500 冊

True Face of the Dalai Lama
——Playing around with all women in the world

Editors/Authors: Pai, Chih-Wei; Wu, Chen-Sheng; Hsin, Tsai-Tsun; Yeh, Yin-Tsan; Cheng, Chung-Hui;
　　　　　　　　Tung, Chien-Chang; Wu, Hsi-Kun
Publisher: True Wisdom Publishing Center
Address: 10th Fl., No. 267, Sec. 3, Chengde Rd., Taipei 10367, Taiwan, R.O.C.
Telephone: 886-2-2595-7295 ext.10-21 (at night / Taipei time)
FAX: 886-2-2595-4493
Domestic Price: NTD 800
Overseas Price: USD 45.00
Edition and Date: 1st Edition, 1st print, 2011/1/31, 1500 copies
Edition and Date: 1st Edition, 2nd print, 2011/6/15, 1500 copies